TABLE OF CONTENTS

Top 20 Test Taking Tips

1. Carefully follow all the test registration procedures
2. Know the test directions, duration, topics, question types, how many questions
3. Setup a flexible study schedule at least 3-4 weeks before test day
4. Study during the time of day you are most alert, relaxed, and stress free
5. Maximize your learning style; visual learner use visual study aids, auditory learner use auditory study aids
6. Focus on your weakest knowledge base
7. Find a study partner to review with and help clarify questions
8. Practice, practice, practice
9. Get a good night's sleep; don't try to cram the night before the test
10. Eat a well balanced meal
11. Know the exact physical location of the testing site; drive the route to the site prior to test day
12. Bring a set of ear plugs; the testing center could be noisy
13. Wear comfortable, loose fitting, layered clothing to the testing center; prepare for it to be either cold or hot during the test
14. Bring at least 2 current forms of ID to the testing center
15. Arrive to the test early; be prepared to wait and be patient
16. Eliminate the obviously wrong answer choices, then guess the first remaining choice
17. Pace yourself; don't rush, but keep working and move on if you get stuck
18. Maintain a positive attitude even if the test is going poorly
19. Keep your first answer unless you are positive it is wrong
20. Check your work, don't make a careless mistake

Math

Do not be intimidated by the questions presented on the math exam. They do not require highly advanced math knowledge, but only the ability to recognize basic problems types and apply simple formulas and methods to solving them. That is our goal, to show you the simple formulas and methods to solving these problems, so that while you will not gain a mastery of math from this guide, you will learn the methods necessary to succeed on the ITBS.

Solving for Variables

Variables are letters that represent an unknown number. You must solve what that number is in single variable problems. The main thing to remember is that you can do anything to one side of an equation as long as you do it to the other.

Example: Solve for x in the equation $2x + 3 = 5$.

Answer: First you want to get the "2x" isolated by itself on one side. To do that, first get rid of the 3. Subtract 3 from both sides of the equation $2x + 3 - 3 = 5 - 3$ or $2x = 2$. Now since the x is being multiplied by the 2 in "2x", you must divide by 2 to get rid of it. So, divide both sides by 2, which gives $2x / 2 = 2 / 2$ or $x = 1$.

Positive/Negative Numbers

Multiplication/Division

A negative multiplied or divided by a negative = a positive number.

Example: $-3 * -4 = 12$; $-6 / -3 = 2$

A negative multiplied by a positve = a negative number.

Example: $-3 * 4 = -12$; $-6 / 3 = -2$

Addition/Subtraction

Treat a negative sign just like a subtraction sign.

Example: $3 + -2 = 3 - 2$ or 1

Remember that you can reverse the numbers while adding or subtracting.

Example: -4+2 = 2 + -4 = 2 – 4 = -2

A negative number subtracted from another number is the same as adding a positive number.

Example: 2 - -1 = 2 + 1 = 3

Beware of making a simple mistake!

Example: An outdoor thermometer drops from 42º to – 8º. By how many degrees has the outside air cooled?

Answer: A common mistake is to say 42º – 8º = 34º, but that is wrong. It is actually 42º - - 8º or 42º + 8º = 50º

Exponents

When exponents are multiplied together, the exponents are added to get the final result.

Example: $x*x = x^2$, where x^1 is implied and $1 + 1 = 2$.

When exponents in parentheses have an exponent, the exponents are multiplied to get the final result.

Example: $(x^3)^2 = x^6$, because $3*2 = 6$.

Another way to think of this is that $(x^3)^2$ is the same as $(x^3)* (x^3)$. Now you can use the multiplication rule given above and add the exponents, $3 + 3 = 6$, so $(x^3)^2 = x^6$

Decimal Exponents (AKA Scientific Notation)

This usually involves converting back and forth between scientific notation and decimal numbers (e.g. 0.02 is the same as 2×10^{-2}). There's an old "cheat" to this problem: if the number is less than 1, the number of digits behind the decimal point is the same as the exponent that 10 is raised to in scientific notation, except that the exponent is a negative number; if the number is greater than 1, the exponent of 10 is equal to the number of digits ahead of the decimal point minus 1.

Example: Convert 3000 to decimal notation.

Answer: 3×10^3, since 4 digits are ahead of the decimal, the number is greater than 1, and $(4-1) = 3$.

Example: Convert 0.05 to decimal notation.

Answer: 5×10^{-2}, since the five is two places behind the decimal (remember, the exponent is negative for numbers less than 1).

Any number raised to an exponent of zero is always 1. Also, unless you know what you're doing, always convert scientific notation to "regular" decimal numbers before doing arithmetic, and convert the answer back if necessary to answer the problem.

Area, Volume, and Surface Area

You can count on questions about area, volume, and surface area to be a significant part of the ITBS. Your best bet is to just memorize the formulas for test day. A list is provided in the appendix for your convenience.

Percents

A percent can be converted to a decimal simply by dividing it by 100.

Example: What is 2% of 50?

Answer: 2% = 2/100 or .02, so .02 * 50 = 1

Word Problems

Some word problems involve percents.

Example: Ticket sales for this year's annual concert at Minutemaid Park were $125,000. The promoter is predicting that next year's sales, in dollars, will be 40% greater than this year's. How many dollars in ticket sales is the promoter predicting for next year?

Answer: Next year's is 40% greater. 40% = 40/100 = .4, so .4 * $125,000 = $50,000. However, the example stated that next year's would be greater by that amount, so next year's sales would be this year's at $125,000 plus the increase at $50,000. $125,000 + $50,000 = $175,000

Some word problems involve distances.

Example: In a certain triangle, the longest side is 1 foot longer than the second-longest side, and the second-longest side is 1 foot longer than the shortest side. If the perimeter is 30 feet, how many feet long is the shortest side.

Answer: There are three sides, let's call them A, B, and C. A is the longest, B the medium sized, and C the shortest. Because A is described in reference to B's length and B is described in reference to C's length, all calculations should be done off of C, the final reference. Use a variable to represent C's length, "x". This means that C is "x" long, B is "x + 1" because B was 1 foot longer than C, and A is "x + 1 + 1" because A was 1 foot longer than B. To calculate a perimeter you simply add all three sides together, so P = length A + length B + length C, or $(x) + (x + 1) + (x + 1 + 1) = x + x + x + 1 + 1 + 1 = 3x + 3$. You know that the perimeter equals 30 feet, so $3x + 3 = 30$. Subtracting 3 from both sides gives $3x + 3 - 3 = 30 - 3$ or $3x = 27$. Dividing both sides by 3 to get "x" all by itself gives $3x / 3 = 27 / 3$ or $x = 9$. So $C = x = 9$, and $B = x + 1 = 9 + 1 = 10$, and $A = x + 1 + 1 = 9 + 1 + 1 = 11$. A quick check of $9 + 10 + 11 = 30$ for the perimeter distance proves that the answer of $x = 9$ is correct

Some word problems involve ratios.

Example: An architect is drawing a scaled blueprint of an apartment building that is to be 100 feet wide and 250 feet long. On the drawing, if the building is 25 inches long, how many inches wide should it be.

Answer: Recognize the word "scaled" to indicate a similar drawing. Similar drawings or shapes can be solved using ratios. First, create the ratio fraction for the missing number, in this case the number of inches wide the drawing should be. The numerator of the first ratio fraction will be the matching known side, in this case "100 feet" wide. The question "100 feet wide is to how many inches wide?" gives us the first fraction of 100 / x. The question "250 feet long is to 25 inches long?" gives us the second fraction of 250 / 25. Again, note that both numerators (100 and 250) are from the same shape. The denominators ("x" and 25) are both from the same shape or drawing as well. Cross multiplication gives 100 * 25 = 250 * x or 2500 = 250x. Dividing both sides by 250 to get x by itself yields 2500 / 250 = 250x / 250 or 10 = x.

Special Formulas

FOIL (First, Outer, Inner, Last)

When you are given a problem such as $(x + 2)(x - 3)$, you should use the FOIL method of multiplication. First, multiply the First parts of each equation $(x*x)$. Then multiply the Outer parts of each equation $(x*-3)$. Note that you should treat the minus 3 in the second equation as a negative 3. Then multiply the Inner parts of each equation $(2*x)$. Finally, multiply the Last parts of each equation $(2*-3)$. Once you are finished, add each part together $(x*x)+(x*-3)+(2*x)+(2*-3) = x^2 + -3x + 2x + -6 = x^2 - 3x + 2x - 6 = x^2 - 1x - 6 = x^2 - x - 6$.

Slope-Intercept formula

$y = mx + b$, where m is the slope of the line and b is the y-intercept.

Example: In the (x,y) coordinate plane, what is the slope of the line $2y = x - 4$?

Answer: First this needs to be converted into slope intercept form. Divide both sides by 2, which gives $2y/2 = (x-4)/2$ or $y = x/2 - 2$. $x/2$ is the same as $\frac{1}{2} *x$, so since m in the formula $y = mx+b$ is the slope, then in the equation $y = \frac{1}{2} * x - 2$, $\frac{1}{2}$ is the slope.

Example: In the (x,y) coordinate plane, where does the line $y = 2x - 3$ cross the y-axis?

Answer: In the formula $y = mx + b$, b is the y – intercept, or where the line crosses the y-axis. In this case, b is represented by –3, so –3 is where the line crosses the y-axis.

Example: In the (x , y) coordinate plane, what is the slope of the line $y = x + 2$?

Answer: This is already in the slope intercept form of $y = mx + b$. Whenever x does not have a number in front of it, you can always assume that there is a 1 there.

Therefore, this equation could also be written as y = 1x + 2, which means m = 1, and the slope is 1.

Slope formula

m = (y1 – y2)/(x1 – x2), where m is the slope of the line and two points on the line are given by (x1,y1) and (x2,y2). This can sometimes be remembered by the statement "rise over run", which means that the "y" values represent the "rise" as they are the up and down dimension and the "x" values represent the "run" as they are the side to side dimension.

Example: What is the slope of a line that passes through points (5,1) and (-2, 3).

Answer: m = (y1 – y2)/(x1 – x2) or (1 – 3)/(5 - -2) or –2 / (5 + 2) or –2 / 7

Line Plotting

If you are trying to plot a line, there is an easy way to do it. First convert the line into slope intercept form (y = mx + b). Then, put a dot on the y-axis at the value of b. For example, if you have a line given by y= 2/3x + 1, then the first point on the line would be at (0,1), because 1 is the y-intercept, or where the line crosses the y-axis. To find the next point on the line, use the slope, which is 2/3. First go 2 increments up, and then 3 increments to the right. To find the next point on the line, go 2 more increments up, and then 3 more increments to the right. You should always go either up or down depending on the numerator in the slope fraction. So if the slope is 3/5, then the numerator is 3, and you should go 3 increments up and 5 increments to the right. You should always go to the right the amount of the denominator. So if the slope is –2, then first you should remember that –2 is the same as –2/1. Since –2 is the denominator, you should go down 2 increments and then 1 increment to the right.

Remember that positive slopes slope upward from left to right and that negative slopes slope downward from left to right.

Simple Probability

The probability problems on the ITBS are fairly straightforward. The basic idea is this: the probability that something will happen is the number of possible ways that something can happen divided by the total number of possible ways for all things that can happen.

Example: I have 20 balloons, 12 are red, 8 are yellow. I give away one yellow balloon; if the next balloon is randomly picked, what is the probability that it will be yellow?

Answer: The probability is 7/19, because after giving one away, there are 7 different ways that the "something" can happen, divided 19 remaining possibilities.

Ratios

When a question asks about two similar shapes, expect a ratio problem.

Example: The figure below shows 2 triangles, where triangle ABC ~ A'B'C'. In these similar triangles, a = 3, b = 4, c = 5, and a' = 6. What is the value of b'?

Answer: You are given the dimensions of 1 side that is similar on both triangles (a and a'). You are looking for b' and are given the dimensions of b. Therefore you can set up a ratio of a/a' = b/b' or 3/6 = 4/b'. To solve, cross multiply the two sides, multiplying 6*4 = 3*b' or 24 = 3b'. Dividing both sides by 3 (24/3 = 3b'/3) makes 8 = b', so 8 is the answer.

Note many other problems may have opportunities to use a ratio. Look for problems where you are trying to find dimensions for a shape and you have dimensions for a similar shape. These can nearly always be solved by setting up a ratio. Just be careful and set up corresponding measurements in the ratios. First decide what you are being asked for on shape B, represented by a variable, such as x. Then ask yourself, which side on similar A is the same size side as x. That is your first ratio fraction, set up a fraction like 2/x if 2 is the similar size side on shape A. Then find a side on each shape that is similar. If 4 is the size of another side on shape A and it corresponds to a side with size 3 on shape B, then your second ratio fraction is 4/3. Note that 2 and 4 are the two numerators in the ratio fractions and are both from shape A. Also note that "x" the unknown side and 3 are both the denominators in the ratio fractions and are both from shape B.

Graphs

Midpoints

To find a midpoint, find the difference in the x-direction between the two endpoints given, and divide by two. Then add that number to the leftmost endpoint's x coordinate. That will be the x coordinate of the midpoint. Next find the difference in the y-direction between the two endpoints given, and divide by two. Then add that number to the lower endpoint's y coordinate. That will be the y coordinate of the midpoint.

Example: What is the midpoint of the line segment with endpoints of (-2 , 5) and (4 , 1)?

Answer: First, subtract the leftmost endpoint's x coordinate from the rightmost endpoint's x coordinate 4 - -2 = 4 + 2 = 6. Then divide by two, 6 / 2 = 3. Then add that number to the leftmost x coordinate -2 + 3 = 1, which is the midpoint's x coordinate. Second, subtract the lower endpoint's y coordinate from the higher endpoint's y coordinate 5 – 1 = 4. Then divide by two, 4 / 2 = 2. Then add that number to the lower y coordinate 1 + 2 = 3, which is the midpoint's y coordinate. So the midpoint is given by (1 , 3).

Angles

If you have a two intersecting lines, remember that the sum of all of the angles can only be 360°. In fact, the two angles on either side of each line will add up to 180°. In the example below, on either side of each line, there is a 137° angle and a 43° angle (137° + 43°) = 180°. Also note that opposite angles are equal. For example, the 43° angle is matched by a similar 43° angle on the opposite side of the intersection.

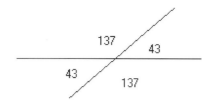

Additionally, parallel lines intersected by a third line will share angles. In the example below, note how each 128° angle is matched by a 128° angle on the opposite side. Also, all of the other angles in this example are 52° angles, because all of the angles on one side of a line have to equal 180° and since there are only two angles, if you have the degree of one, then you can find the degree of the other. In this case, the missing angle is given by 180° – 128° = 52°.

Finally, remember that all of the angles in a triangle will add up to 180°. If you are given two of the angles, then subtract them both from 180° and you will have the degree of the third missing angle.

Example: If you have a triangle with two given angles of 20° and 130°, what degree is the third angle?

Answer: All angles must add up to 180°, so 180° – 20° – 130° = 30°.

Right Triangles

Whenever you see the words "right triangle" or "90° angle," alarm bells should go off. These problems will almost always involve the law of right triangles, AKA The Pythagorean Theorem:

$A^2 + B^2 = C^2$

Where A = the length of one of the shorter sides

B = the length of the other shorter side

C = the length of the hypotenuse or longest side opposite the 90° angle

MAKE SURE YOU KNOW THIS FORMULA. At least 3-5 questions will reference variations on this formula by giving you two of the three variables and asking you to solve for the third.

Example: A right triangle has sides of 3 and 4; what is the length of the hypotenuse?

Answer: Solving the equation, $A^2=9$, $B^2=16$, so $C^2=25$; the square root of 25 is 5, the length of the hypotenuse C.

Example: In the rectangle below, what is the length of the diagonal line?

Answer: This rectangle is actually made of two right triangles. Whenever you have a right triangle, the Pythagorean Theorem can be used. Since the right side of the triangle is equal to 5, then the left side must also be equal to 5. This creates a triangle with one side equal to 5 and another side equal to 8. To use the Pythagorean Theorem, we state that $5^2 + 8^2 = C^2$ or $25 + 64 = C^2$ or $89 = C^2$ or C = Square Root of 89

Circles

Many students have never seen the formula for a circle:

$(x-A)^2 + (y-B)^2 = r^2$

This looks intimidating, but it's really not:

A = the coordinate of the center on the x-axis

B = the coordinate of the center on the y-axis

r = the radius of the circle

Example: What is the radius of the circle described by: $(x+2)^2 + (x-3)^2 = 16$

Answer: Since $r^2 = 16$, r, the radius, equals 4.

Also, this circle is centered at (-2,3) since those must be the values of A and B in the generic equation to make it the same as this equation.

Plug and Chug

Sometimes when faced by a problem containing variables that are confusing, replace the variables with some made up numbers, then test those numbers with your calculator to come up with an answer.

Sometimes you can also plug each of the answer choices in and see which one is right. Let your calculator work for you.

Final Note

Even if you did well in math in high school, you may not succeed on the ITBS. While math tests in high school test specific competencies in specific subjects, the ITBS frequently tests your ability to apply math concepts from vastly different math subjects in one problem. However, in few cases is any ITBS math problem more than two "layers" deep.

What does this mean for you? You can easily learn the ITBS Math through taking multiple practice tests. If you have some gaps in your math knowledge, we suggest you buy a more basic study guide to help you build a foundation before applying our secrets. Check out our special report to find out which books are worth your time.

Reading

Skimming

Your first task when you begin reading is to answer the question "What is the topic of the selection?" This can best be answered by quickly skimming the passage for the general idea, stopping to read only the first sentence of each paragraph. A paragraph's first is usually the main topic sentence, and it gives you a summary of the content of the paragraph.

Once you've skimmed the passage, stopping to read only the first sentences, you will have a general idea about what it is about, as well as what is the expected topic in each paragraph.

Each question will contain clues as to where to find the answer in the passage. Do not just randomly search through the passage for the correct answer to each question. Search scientifically. Find key word(s) or ideas in the question that are going to either contain or be near the correct answer. These are typically nouns, verbs, numbers, or phrases in the question that will probably be duplicated in the passage. Once you have identified those key word(s) or idea, skim the passage quickly to find where those key word(s) or idea appears. The correct answer choice will be nearby.

Example: What caused Martin to suddenly return to Paris?

The key word is Paris. Skim the passage quickly to find where this word appears. The answer will be close by that word.

However, sometimes key words in the question are not repeated in the passage. In those cases, search for the general idea of the question.

Example: Which of the following was the psychological impact of the author's childhood upon the remainder of his life?

Key words are "childhood" or "psychology". While searching for those words, be alert for other words or phrases that have similar meaning, such as "emotional effect" or "mentally" which could be used in the passage, rather than the exact word "psychology".

Numbers or years can be particularly good key words to skim for, as they stand out from the rest of the text.

Example: Which of the following best describes the influence of Monet's work in the 20th century?

20th contains numbers and will easily stand out from the rest of the text. Use 20th as the key word to skim for in the passage.

Other good key word(s) may be in quotation marks. These identify a word or phrase that is copied directly from the passage. In those cases, the word(s) in quotation marks are exactly duplicated in the passage.

Example: In her college years, what was meant by Margaret's "drive for excellence"?

"Drive for excellence" is a direct quote from the passage and should be easy to find.

Once you've quickly found the correct section of the passage to find the answer, focus upon the answer choices. Sometimes a choice will repeat word for word a portion of the passage near the answer. However, beware of such duplication – it may be a trap! More than likely, the correct choice will paraphrase or summarize the related portion of the passage, rather than being exactly the same wording.

For the answers that you think are correct, read them carefully and make sure that they answer the question. An answer can be factually correct, but it MUST answer the question asked. Additionally, two answers can both be seemingly correct, so be sure to read all of the answer choices, and make sure that you get the one that BEST answers the question.

Some questions will not have a key word.

Example: Which of the following would the author of this passage likely agree with?

In these cases, look for key words in the answer choices. Then skim the passage to find where the answer choice occurs. By skimming to find where to look, you can minimize the time required.

Sometimes it may be difficult to identify a good key word in the question to skim for in the passage. In those cases, look for a key word in one of the answer choices to skim for. Often the answer choices can all be found in the same paragraph, which can quickly narrow your search.

Paragraph Focus

Focus upon the first sentence of each paragraph, which is the most important. The main topic of the paragraph is usually there.

Once you've read the first sentence in the paragraph, you have a general idea about what each paragraph will be about. As you read the questions, try to determine which paragraph will have the answer. Paragraphs have a concise topic. The answer should either obviously be there or obviously not. It will save time if you can jump straight to the paragraph, so try to remember what you learned from the first sentences.

Example: The first paragraph is about poets; the second is about poetry. If a question asks about poetry, where will the answer be? The second paragraph.

The main idea of a passage is typically spread across all or most of its paragraphs. Whereas the main idea of a paragraph may be completely different than the main idea of the very next paragraph, a main idea for a passage affects all of the paragraphs in one form or another.

Example: What is the main idea of the passage?

For each answer choice, try to see how many paragraphs are related. It can help to count how many sentences are affected by each choice, but it is best to see how many paragraphs are affected by the choice. Typically the answer choices will include incorrect choices that are main ideas of individual paragraphs, but not the entire passage. That is why it is crucial to choose ideas that are supported by the most paragraphs possible.

Eliminate Choices

Some choices can quickly be eliminated. "Andy Warhol lived there." Is Andy Warhol even mentioned in the article? If not, quickly eliminate it.

When trying to answer a question such as "the passage indicates all of the following EXCEPT" quickly skim the paragraph searching for references to each choice. If the reference exists, scratch it off as a choice. Similar choices may be crossed off simultaneously if they are close enough.

In choices that ask you to choose "which answer choice does NOT describe?" or "all of the following answer choices are identifiable characteristics, EXCEPT which?" look for answers that are similarly worded. Since only one answer can be correct, if there are two answers that appear to mean the same thing, they must BOTH be incorrect, and can be eliminated.

Example Answer Choices:

A.)   changing values and attitudes

B.)   a large population of mobile or uprooted people

These answer choices are similar; they both describe a fluid culture. Because of their similarity, they can be linked together. Since the answer can have only one choice, they can also be eliminated together.

When presented with a question that offers two choices, or neither choice, or both choice, it is rarely both choices.

Example: When an atom emits a beta particle, the mass of the atom will:

A.   increase

B.   decrease.

C.   stay the same.

D.   either increase or decrease depending on conditions.

Answer D will rarely be correct, the answers are usually more concrete.

Contextual Clues

Look for contextual clues. An answer can be right but not correct. The contextual clues will help you find the answer that is most right and is correct. Understand the context in which a phrase is stated.

When asked for the implied meaning of a statement made in the passage, immediately go find the statement and read the context it was made in. Also, look for an answer choice that has a similar phrase to the statement in question.

Example: In the passage, what is implied by the phrase "Churches have become more or less part of the furniture"?

Find an answer choice that is similar or describes the phrase "part of the furniture" as that is the key phrase in the question. "Part of the furniture" is a saying that means something is fixed, immovable, or set in their ways. Those are all similar ways of saying "part of the furniture." As such, the correct answer choice will probably include a similar rewording of the expression.

Example: Why was John described as "morally desperate".

The answer will probably have some sort of definition of morals in it. "Morals" refers to a code of right and wrong behavior, so the correct answer choice will likely have words that mean something like that.

Fact/Opinion

When asked about which statement is a fact or opinion, remember that answer choices that are facts will typically have no ambiguous words. For example, how long is a long time? What defines an ordinary person? These ambiguous words of "long" and "ordinary" should not be in a factual statement. However, if all of the choices have ambiguous words, go to the context of the passage. Often a factual statement may be set out as a research finding.

Example: "The scientist found that the eye reacts quickly to change in light."

Opinions may be set out in the context of words like thought, believed, understood, or wished.

Example: "He thought the Yankees should win the World Series."

Time Management

In technical passages, do not get lost on the technical terms. Skip them and move on. You want a general understanding of what is going on, not a mastery of the passage.

When you encounter material in the selection that seems difficult to understand, bracket it. It often may not be necessary and can be skipped. Only spend time trying to understand it if it is going to be relevant for a question. Understand difficult phrases only as a last resort.

If low on time, save sequence questions that ask you to sequence four choices (I, II, III, IV) for last. They consume a lot of time. When you do work on them, first find the four sequences in the passages, and mark them I, II, III, and IV respectively. Look for transitional word cues in the sentences such as: first, initially, to start, early on, finally, in conclusion, in the end, or last. These transition words can help position the choices. Also, focus on eliminating the wrong choices. If you know that a certain sequence must be first or last, then you can eliminate the choices that do not have that as an option.

Pace yourself. 9 minutes per passage, which is nearly a minute per question. Do easy passages and questions first. The easier passages should be first.

Answer general questions before detail questions. A reader with a good understanding of the whole passage can often answer general questions without rereading a word. Get the easier questions out of the way before tackling the more time consuming ones.

Identify each question by type. Usually the wording of a question will tell you whether you can find the answer by referring directly to the passage or by using your reasoning powers. You alone know which question types you customarily handle with ease and which give you trouble and will require more time. Save the difficult questions for last.

Warnings

When asked for a conclusion that may be drawn, look for critical "hedge" phrases, such as likely, may, can, will often, sometimes, etc, often, almost, mostly, usually, generally, rarely, sometimes. Question writers insert these hedge phrases, to cover every possibility. Often an answer will be wrong simply because it leaves no room for exception.

Example: Animals live longer in cold places than animals in warm places.

This answer choice is wrong, because there are exceptions in which certain warm climate animals live longer. This answer choice leaves no possibility of exception. It states that every animal species in cold places live longer than animal species in warm places. Correct answer choices will typically have a key hedge word to leave room for exceptions.

Example: In severe cold, a polar bear cub is likely to survive longer than an adult polar bear.

This answer choice is correct, because not only does the passage imply that younger animals survive better in the cold, it also allows for exceptions to exist. The use of the word "likely" leaves room for cases in which a polar bear cub might not survive longer than the adult polar bear.

When asked how a word is used in the passage, don't use your existing knowledge of the word. The question is being asked precisely because there is some strange or unusual usage of the word in the passage. Go to the passage and use contextual

- 25 -

clues to determine the answer. Don't simply use the popular definition you already know.

Stay alert for "switchbacks". These are the words and phrases frequently used to alert you to shifts in thought. The most common switchback word is "but". Others include although, however, nevertheless, on the other hand, even though, while, in spite of, despite, regardless of.

Once you know which paragraph the answer will be in, focus on that paragraph. However, don't get distracted by a choice that is factually true about the paragraph. Your search is for the answer that answers the question, which may be about a tiny aspect in the paragraph. Stay focused and don't fall for an answer that describes the larger picture of the paragraph. Always go back to the question and make sure you're choosing an answer that actually answers the question and is not just a true statement.

Science

Answer Choice Elimination Techniques

Slang

Scientific sounding answers are better than slang ones. In the answer choices below, choice B is much less scientific and is incorrect, while choice A is a scientific analytical choice and is correct.

Example:

a.) To compare the outcomes of the two different kinds of treatment.

b.) Because some subjects insisted on getting one or the other of the treatments.

Extreme Statements

Avoid wild answers that throw out highly controversial ideas that are proclaimed as established fact. Choice A is a radical idea and is incorrect. Choice B is a calm rational statement. Notice that Choice B does not make a definitive, uncompromising stance, using a hedge word "if" to provide wiggle room.

Example:

a.) Bypass surgery should be discontinued completely.

b.) Medication should be used instead of surgery for patients who have not had a heart attack if they suffer from mild chest pain and mild coronary artery blockage.

Similar Answer Choices

When you have two answer choices that are direct opposites, one of them is usually the correct answer.

Example:

A.) The effectiveness of enzyme I at 30 degrees Celsius depends on its concentration.

- 27 -

B.) The effectiveness of enzyme II at 30 degrees Celsius depends on its concentration.

These two answer choices are very similar and fall into the same family of answer choices. A family of answer choices is when two or three answer choices are very similar. Often two will be opposites and one may show an equality.
Example:

A.) Operation I or Operation II can be conducted at equal cost
B.) Operation I would be less expensive than Operation II
C.) Operation II would be less expensive than Operation I
D.) Neither Operation I nor Operation II would be effective at preventing the spread of cancer.

Note how the first three choices are all related. They all ask about a cost comparison. Beware of immediately recognizing choices B and C as opposites and choosing one of those two. Choice A is in the same family of questions and should be considered as well. However, choice D is not in the same family of questions. It has nothing to do with cost and can be discounted in most cases.

Related to the family of answers concept are answer choices that have similar parts.
Example:

A.) The first stage of reaction 1 and the first stage of reaction 2.
B.) The second stage of reaction 1 and the second stage of reaction 3.
C.) The second stage of reaction 1 and the second stage of reaction 2.
D.) The second stage of reaction 1 and the first stage of reaction 2.

In this question, answer choices B, C, and D all begin with the same phrase "the second stage of reaction 1". This means answer choice A can be eliminated. Then answer choices A and D both have the same phrase "the first stage of reaction 2". Also, answer choices B and C have different phrases. This means that either A or D is the correct answer. Since choice A has already been eliminated, D is probably the right answer. In these cases similar phrases identify answer choices as being members of the same family of answers. Each answer choice that has a similar phrase is in the same family of answers. Answer choices that fall into the most family of answers is usually the correct answer.

Once again, hedge words are usually good, while answer choices without hedge words are typically wrong. Answer choices that say "exactly", "always" are often wrong.

Time Management

Scan the passage to get a rough idea of what it is asking.

Avoid answers that while they are obviously true they don't answer the question. Answers must ANSWER the question, not just be factually true statements. The answer choice must be based strictly on the contents of the passage and question.

Read all the choices. Later answer choices will often bring up a new point that you may not have considered. As you read the choices, scratch through the ones that you know are wrong, but don't make your final selection until you read them all.

The easier "understanding" questions are listed first. Do not skip these first questions in each group, though everywhere else (on other tests and in other questions in the science test that aren't the first question in a group) skip questions giving you too much difficulty. This is because if you don't understand the passage, you're in trouble on the latter questions. Make sure you know enough to get the first question right, because the other questions will all flow from a basic understanding of the passage.

Skip the hard questions that aren't the first question in a group.

If the answers are numerical, estimate. Calculation takes time, and you should avoid it whenever possible. You can usually eliminate three obviously wrong choices quite easily. For example, suppose a graph shows that an object has traveled 48 meters in 11 seconds, and you are asked to find its speed. You are given these choices:

a. 250 m/s
b. 42 m/s
c. 4.4 m/s
d. 1.2 m/s

You know that 48 divided by 11 will be a little over 4, so you can pick out C as the answer without ever doing the calculation.

Highly Technical Questions May Not Be

Sometimes a single piece of information may be given to you. For example, blood velocity is lowest in the capillaries (averaging 3cm/sec).
A question may ask the following:
A physician examining a newly discovered tribe of people deep in the Amazon jungles found that the relative total surface area of their capillaries was greater than that previously reported for any other people. If the physician were to predict the average velocity of blood through their capillaries, which of the following values would be the most reasonable.

A.) 2 cm/sec
B.) 3 cm/sec
C.) 4 cm/sec

D.) 5 cm/sec

You know that 3 cm/sec is the standard, which is choice B. Without understanding any of the subject matter or even reading the associated graph, it is possible to choose the correct answer, which is A. The reason is because there is only answer, which is less than 3 cm/sec, while there are two answers that are greater than 3 cm/sec. Since you are not looking for an exact answer, but only a reasonable answer, then you can conclude that if the correct answer was greater than 3 cm/sec, TWO answer choices would meet that criteria. However, if the correct answer is less than 3 cm/sec, only ONE answer choice meets that criteria, meaning it is likely the correct answer.

Experiment Passages

The best way to remember three different but similar experiments is to focus on the differences between the experiments. Between the first and second experiment, what was changed? Between the second and third experiment, what was done differently? That will keep the overall experiments properly aligned in your mind. What variables changed between the experiments?

Random Tips

- On fact questions that require choosing between numbers, don't guess the smallest or largest choice unless you're sure of the answer (remember- "sure" means you would bet $5 on it).

- Short answer questions want you to choose between several words that are choices. Your best weapon on these is process of elimination- there are no easy tips.

- The long answer questions will often have a few "bizarre" choices, mentioning things that are not relevant to the passage. Also avoid answers that sound "smart." Again, if you're willing to bet $5, disregard the tips and go with your bet.

- In passages that describe a series of experiments, often the questions will ask you if the researcher made a mistake, or could improve the experiments by making some change; the answer choices will be two yes's and two no's, each with a different justification. Usually, the answer is one of the "no" choices- ITBS does not include deliberately flawed experiments in passages, so it is safe to assume that whatever suggestion the question poses would NOT improve the experiment. Of course, if you KNOW ($5 confidence) otherwise, disregard the tip.
- This bears repeating, especially on this test: you have probably never had a science test quite like this. More than any other test, you MUST take at least one practice test so as to not be bogged down with the unfamiliar format.

Biology

Molecular and Cellular Biology

Chemical Basis of Life

Atom- A unit of matter, the smallest unit of an element, having all the characteristics of that element and consisting of a dense, central, positively charged nucleus surrounded by a system of electrons

Molecule- The smallest particle of a substance that retains the chemical and physical properties of the substance and is composed of two or more atoms; a group of like or different atoms held together by chemical forces

Chemical Bond- Any of several forces or mechanisms, especially the ionic bond, covalent bond, and metallic bond, by which atoms or ions are bound in a molecule or crystal

Neutron- An electrically neutral subatomic particle in the baryon family, having a mass 1,839 times that of the electron, stable when bound in an atomic nucleus, and having a mean lifetime of approximately 1.0×10^3 seconds as a free particle. It and the proton form nearly the entire mass of atomic nuclei.

Proton- A stable, positively charged subatomic particle in the baryon family having a mass 1,836 times that of the electron.

Electron- A stable subatomic particle in the lepton family having a rest mass of 9.1066×10^{-28} grams and a unit negative electric charge of approximately 1.602×10^{-19} coulombs

Atomic Number- The number of protons in an atomic nucleus

Isotope- One of two or more atoms having the same atomic number but different mass numbers

Radioactivity- Spontaneous emission of radiation, either directly from unstable atomic nuclei or as a consequence of a nuclear reaction

Covalent bond- A chemical bond formed by the sharing of one or more electrons, especially pairs of electrons, between atoms

Ionic bond- A chemical bond between two ions with opposite charges, characteristic of salts

Hydrogen bond- A chemical bond in which a hydrogen atom of one molecule is attracted to an electronegative atom, especially a nitrogen, oxygen, or fluorine atom, usually of another molecule

pH- p(otential of) H(ydrogen); the logarithm of the reciprocal of hydrogen-ion concentration in gram atoms per liter; used as a measure of the acidity or alkalinity of a solution on a scale of 0-14 (where 7 is neutral)

Know the structure and function of biologically important molecules. Also know the unique features of water.

Know the following organic molecules:

Amino acids- An organic compound containing an amino group (NH_2), a carboxylic acid group (COOH), and any of various side groups, especially any of the 20 compounds that have the basic formula $NH_2CHRCOOH$, and that link together by peptide bonds to form proteins or that function as chemical messengers and as intermediates in metabolism

Proteins- Any of a group of complex organic macromolecules that contain carbon, hydrogen, oxygen, nitrogen, and usually sulfur and are composed of one or more chains of amino acids. Proteins are fundamental components of all living cells and include many substances, such as enzymes, hormones, and antibodies, that are necessary for the proper functioning of an organism.

Nucleotides- Any of various compounds consisting of a nucleoside combined with a phosphate group and forming the basic constituent of DNA and RNA

Nucleic acids- Any of a group of complex compounds found in all living cells and viruses, composed of purines, pyrimidines, carbohydrates, and phosphoric acid. Nucleic acids in the form of DNA and RNA control cellular function and heredity

Thermodynamics- Physics that deals with the relationships and conversions between heat and other forms of energy.

Anabolic- The phase of metabolism in which simple substances are synthesized into the complex materials of living tissue.

Catabolic- The metabolic breakdown of complex molecules into simpler ones, often resulting in a release of energy

Endergomic- Requiring energy

Exergonic- Releasing energy

Enzymes- Any of numerous proteins or conjugated proteins produced by living organisms and functioning as biochemical catalysts

Coenzymes- A nonproteinaceous organic substance that usually contains a vitamin or mineral and combines with a specific protein, the apoenzyme, to form an active enzyme system

Photosynthesis- The process in green plants and certain other organisms by which carbohydrates are synthesized from carbon dioxide and water using light as an energy source. Most forms of photosynthesis release oxygen as a byproduct.

Cellular Respiration- The series of metabolic processes by which living cells produce energy through the oxidation of organic substances.

Aerobic - Living or occurring only in the presence of oxygen

Anaerobic- An organism, such as a bacterium, that can live in the absence of atmospheric oxygen

Cell Structure and Function

Nucleus- A large, membrane-bound, usually spherical protoplasmic structure within a living cell, containing the cell's hereditary material and controlling its metabolism, growth, and reproduction

Organelles- A differentiated structure within a cell, such as a mitochondrion, vacuole, or chloroplast that performs a specific function.

Nucleolus- A small, typically round granular body composed of protein and RNA in the nucleus of a cell. It is usually associated with a specific chromosomal site and involved in ribosomal RNA synthesis and the formation of ribosomes.

Ribosome- A minute round particle composed of RNA and protein that is found in the cytoplasm of living cells and serves as the site of assembly for polypeptides encoded by messenger RNA.

Smooth Endoplasmic Reticulum- An internal membrane structure of the eukaryotic cell. Biochemically similar to the rough endoplasmic reticulum, but lacks the ribosome binding function

Rough Endoplasmic Reticulum- Membrane organelle of eukaryotes that forms sheets and tubules

Golgi Apparatus- A network of stacked membranous vesicles present in most living cells that functions in the formation of secretions within the cell

Lysosomes- A membrane-bound organelle in the cytoplasm of most cells containing various hydrolytic enzymes that function in intracellular digestion

Vacuoles- A small cavity in the cytoplasm of a cell, bound by a single membrane and containing water, food, or metabolic waste

Mitochondria- A spherical or elongated organelle in the cytoplasm of nearly all eukaryotic cells, containing genetic material and many enzymes important for cell metabolism, including those responsible for the conversion of food to usable energy

Chloroplasts- A chlorophyll-containing plastid found in algal and green plant cells

Cytoskeleton- The internal framework of a cell, composed largely of actin filaments and microtubules

Microvilli- Any of the minute hairlike structures projecting from the surface of certain types of epithelial cells, especially those of the small intestine.

Flagella- A long, threadlike appendage, especially a whiplike extension of certain cells or unicellular organisms that functions as an organ of locomotion

Cilium- A microscopic hairlike process extending from the surface of a cell or unicellular organism. Capable of rhythmical motion, it acts in unison with other such structures to bring about the movement of the cell or of the surrounding medium

Prokaryotic- An organism of the kingdom Monera (or Prokaryotae), comprising the bacteria and cyanobacteria, characterized by the absence of a distinct, membrane-bound nucleus or membrane-bound organelles, and by DNA that is not organized into chromosomes

Eukaryotic- A single-celled or multicellular organism whose cells contain a distinct membrane-bound nucleus

Homeostasis- The ability or tendency of an organism or cell to maintain internal equilibrium by adjusting its physiological processes

Meiosis- The process of cell division in sexually reproducing organisms that reduces the number of chromosomes in reproductive cells from diploid to haploid, leading to the production of gametes in animals and spores in plants

Know the Cell Cycle.

Molecular Basis of Heredity

Heredity- The genetic transmission of characteristics from parent to offspring.

Genetics- The branch of biology that deals with heredity, especially the mechanisms of hereditary transmission and the variation of inherited characteristics among similar or related organisms.

Deoxyribonucletides

A nitrogen-containing ring structure called a **base**. The base is attached to the 1' carbon atom of the pentose. In DNA, four different bases are found:

1. two purines, called adenine (A) and guanine (G)
2. two pyrimidines, called thymine (T) and cytosine (C)

Ribonuceotides-

RNA contains:

1. The same purines, adenine (A) and guanine (G).

2. RNA also uses the pyrimidine cytosine (C), but instead of thymine, it uses the pyrimidine uracil (U).

Cloning- A DNA sequence, such as a gene, that is transferred from one organism to another and replicated by genetic engineering techniques

Genetics and Evolution

Evolution-

    a. Change in the genetic composition of a population during successive generations, as a result of natural selection acting on the genetic variation among individuals, and resulting in the development of new species.

    b. The historical development of a related group of organisms; phylogeny

Charles Darwin- British naturalist who revolutionized the study of biology with his theory of evolution based on natural selection

Hardy-Weinberg (& Castle) Theorem

1908, G. H. Hardy and W. Weinberg and W. Castle independently disproved the naive supposition that by numerical prevalence, an allele will become more common through time (i.e., gene frequencies change on their own, randomly)

In the absence of evolutionary processes, gene frequencies will stay the same through time

Several assumptions are made:

- No mutation
- No migration
- No selection
- No inbreeding (i.e., an infinitely large population)
- No drift (i.e. same as above)
- Completely random mating

Three points made by the H-W theorem:

1) Allele frequencies do not change from one generation to the next

2) Equilibrium genotype frequencies do not change and are given by the H-W formula

3) Equilibrium is attained in a single generation (if the allele frequencies are the same in both sexes)

Natural Selection- The process in nature by which, according to Darwin's theory of evolution, only the organisms best adapted to their environment tend to survive and transmit their genetic characteristics in increasing numbers to succeeding generations while those less adapted tend to be eliminated

Speciation- The evolutionary formation of new biological species, usually by the division of a single species into two or more genetically distinct ones

Hybrid- The offspring of genetically dissimilar parents or stock, especially the offspring produced by breeding plants or animals of different varieties, species, or races

Extinction-

      a. Change in the genetic composition of a population during successive generations, as a result of natural selection acting on the genetic variation among individuals, and resulting in the development of new species.

      b. The historical development of a related group of organisms

Gregor Mendel- Austrian botanist and founder of the science of genetics. Through experiments with plants, chiefly garden peas, he discovered the principle of the inheritance of characteristics through the combination of genes from parent cells.

Law of Segregation- The principles that govern heredity were discovered by a monk named Gregor Mendel in the 1860's. One of these principles, now called Mendel's law of segregation, states that allele pairs separate or segregate during gamete formation, and randomly unite at fertilization

Law of Independent Assortment- The principles that govern heredity were discovered by a monk named Gregor Mendel in the 1860's. One of these principles, now called Mendel's law of independent assortment, states that allele pairs separate independently during the formation of gametes. This means that traits are transmitted to offspring independently of one another.

Alleles- An alternative form of a gene (one member of a pair) that is located at a specific position on a specific chromosome.

Gametes- Haploid reproductive cells that unite during sexual reproduction to form a diploid zygote. Male gametes are sperm and female gametes are eggs.

Haploid-

1. Having the same number of sets of chromosomes as a germ cell or half as many as a somatic cell.
2. Having a single set of chromosomes

Diploid- Having a pair of each type of chromosome, so that the basic chromosome number is doubled

Sex chromosomes- Either of a pair of chromosomes, usually designated X or Y, in the germ cells of most animals and some plants, that combine to determine the sex and sex-linked characteristics of an individual, with XX resulting in a female and XY in a male in mammals

Ecology: Organism and Environments

Population- All the organisms that constitute a specific group or occur in a specified habitat

Community-

a. A group of plants and animals living and interacting with one another in a specific region under relatively similar environmental conditions.
b. The region occupied by a group of interacting organisms.

Diversity- Variety or multiformity

Predation- The capturing of prey as a means of maintaining life

Parasitism- The characteristic behavior or mode of existence of a parasite or parasitic population

Mutualism- An association between organisms of two different species in which each member benefits

Succession- The gradual and orderly process of ecosystem development brought about by changes in community composition and the production of a climax characteristic of a particular geographic region

Ecosystem- An ecological community together with its environment, functioning as a unit

Know the following types, characteristics of and biological diversity within biomes:

Aquatic- Consisting of, relating to, or being in water

Terrestrial- Living or growing on land; not aquatic

Trophic levels:

Producers- A photosynthetic green plant or chemosynthetic bacterium, constituting the first trophic level in a food chain; an autotrophic organism

Consumers- A heterotrophic organism that ingests other organisms or organic matter in a food chain

Decomposers- An organism, often a bacterium or fungus that feeds on and breaks down dead plant or animal matter, thus making organic nutrients available to the ecosystem.

Autotrophs- An organism capable of synthesizing its own food from inorganic substances, using light or chemical energy.

Heterotrophs- An organism that cannot synthesize its own food and is dependent on complex organic substances for nutrition.

Food Chain- A succession of organisms in an ecological community that constitutes a continuation of food energy from one organism to another as each consumes a lower member and in turn is preyed upon by a higher member

Organism Biology and Diversity of Life

Kingdom classification system:

Monera- prokaryotic bacteria and blue-green algae and various primitive pathogens; because of lack of consensus on how to divide the organisms into phyla informal names are used for the major divisions

Protista- A provisional group in which are placed a number of low microscopic organisms of doubtful nature

Fungi- Any of numerous eukaryotic organisms of the kingdom Fungi, which lack chlorophyll and vascular tissue and range in form from a single cell to a body mass of branched filamentous hyphae that often produce specialized fruiting bodies

Plantae- taxonomic kingdom comprising all living or extinct plants

Animalia- taxonomic kingdom comprising all living or extinct animals

Domain Systems:

Bacteria- Any of the unicellular prokaryotic microorganisms of the class **Schizomycetes**, which vary in terms of morphology, oxygen and nutritional requirements, and motility, and may be free-living, saprophytic, or pathogenic in plants or animals

Archaea- This is a super-classification of odd bacteria that are neither prokaryotes nor eukaryotes; some scientists believe they represent a separate kingdom. The primary genus is *Archaebacteria*, whose members fall in three categories: microbes that can live in extremely salty environments (halophiles), microbes that produce methane (methanogens), and microbes that can live in extremely hot environments (thermophiles).

Eukarya- The phylogenetic domain containing all eukaryotic organisms

Nomenclature Schemes are as follows: kingdom, phylum, class, order, family, genus, and species

Plants

Know the evolution of plants

Know the different types of plants

Gymnosperms- A plant, such as a cycad or conifer, whose seeds are not enclosed within an ovary

Bryophytes- A plant of the Bryophyta, a division of photosynthetic, chiefly terrestrial, nonvascular plants, including the mosses, liverworts, and hornworts

Pterophytes- Any of numerous flowerless, seedless vascular plants having roots, stems, and fronds and reproducing by spores

Angiosperms- A plant whose ovules are enclosed in an ovary; a flowering plant

Xylem- The supporting and water-conducting tissue of vascular plants, consisting primarily of tracheids and vessels; woody tissue

Phloem- The food-conducting tissue of vascular plants, consisting of sieve tubes, fibers, parenchyma, and sclereids

Gametophytes- The gamete-producing phase in a plant characterized by alternation of generations

Sporophytes- The spore-producing phase in the life cycle of a plant that exhibits alternation of generations

Germination- The process of germinating; the beginning of vegetation or growth in a seed or plant; the first development of germs, either animal or vegetable

Animals

Know the classification based on phylogeny:

Porifera- The grand division of the animal kingdom which includes the sponges

Cnidaria- A comprehensive group equivalent to the true Coelenterata, i.e. exclusive of the sponges

Platyhelminthes- flatworms

Nematoda- An order of worms, having a long, round, and generally smooth body; the roundworms. They are mostly parasites

Rotifera- An order of minute worms which usually have one or two groups of vibrating cilia on the head, which, when in motion, often give an appearance of rapidly revolving wheels

- 42 -

Mollusca- An invertebrate group with a hard shell and a soft body

Arthropoda- A large division of Articulata, embracing all those that have jointed legs.

Annelida- A division of the Articulata, having the body formed of numerous rings or annular segments, and without jointed legs.

Echinodermata- radially symmetrical marine invertebrates including e.g. starfish and sea urchins and sea cucumbers

Chordate- Any of numerous animals belonging to the phylum Chordata, having at some stage of development a dorsal nerve cord, a notochord, and gill slits and including all vertebrates and certain marine animals, such as the lancelets

Know about circulation of animal systems such as:

Heart- The chambered muscular organ in vertebrates that pumps blood received from the veins into the arteries, thereby maintaining the flow of blood through the entire circulatory system

Blood Vessel- An elastic tubular channel, such as an artery, a vein, or a capillary, through which the blood circulates

Veins- Any of the membranous tubes that form a branching system and carry blood to the heart

Artery- Any of the muscular elastic tubes that form a branching system and that carry blood away from the heart to the cells, tissues, and organs of the body

Capillary- One of the minute blood vessels that connect arterioles and venules. These blood vessels form an intricate network throughout the body for the interchange of various substances, such as oxygen and carbon dioxide, between blood and tissue cells

Digestion- The process by which food is converted into substances that can be absorbed and assimilated by the body. It is accomplished in the alimentary canal by the mechanical and enzymatic breakdown of foods into simpler chemical compounds

Enzymes- Any of numerous proteins or conjugated proteins produced by living organisms and functioning as biochemical catalysts

Cholecystokinin- A hormone produced principally by the small intestine in response to the presence of fats, causing contraction of the gallbladder, release of bile, and secretion of pancreatic digestive enzymes

Gastrin- A hormone secreted by glands in the mucous membrane of the stomach that stimulates the production of gastric juice

Blood- The fluid consisting of plasma, blood cells, and platelets that is circulated by the heart through the vertebrate vascular system, carrying oxygen and nutrients to and waste materials away from all body tissues

Erythrocytes- A cell in the blood of vertebrates that transports oxygen and carbon dioxide to and from the tissues. In mammals, the red blood cell is disk-shaped and biconcave, contains hemoglobin, and lacks a nucleus

Hemoglobin- The iron-containing respiratory pigment in red blood cells of vertebrates, consisting of about 6 percent heme and 94 percent globin

Leukocytes- Any of various blood cells that have a nucleus and cytoplasm, separate into a thin white layer when whole blood is centrifuged, and help protect the body from infection and disease

Plasma- The clear, yellowish fluid portion of blood, lymph, or intramuscular fluid in which cells are suspended. It differs from serum in that it contains fibrin and other soluble clotting elements

Platelets- A minute, nonnucleated, disklike cytoplasmic body found in the blood plasma of mammals that is derived from a megakaryocyte and functions to promote blood clotting

Immunity- The quality or condition of being immune

Antibodies- A Y-shaped protein on the surface of B cells that is secreted into the blood or lymph in response to an antigenic stimulus, such as a bacterium, virus, parasite, or transplanted organ, and that neutralizes the antigen by binding specifically to it; an immunoglobulin

Antigens- A substance that when introduced into the body stimulates the production of an antibody

Thermoregulation- Maintenance of a constant internal body temperature independent from the environmental temperature

Respiration- The act or process of inhaling and exhaling; breathing

Excretion- The act or process of discharging waste matter from the blood, tissues, or organs

Nervous System- The system of cells, tissues, and organs that regulates the body's responses to internal and external stimuli. In vertebrates it consists of the brain, spinal cord, nerves, ganglia, and parts of the receptor and effector organs

Cardiovascular System- (circulatory system) The bodily system consisting of the heart, blood vessels, and blood that circulates blood throughout the body, delivers nutrients and other essential materials to cells, and removes waste products

Endocrine System-The bodily system that consists of the endocrine glands and functions to regulate body activities

Respiratory System- The integrated system of organs involved in the intake and exchange of oxygen and carbon dioxide between an organism and the environment

Digestive System- The alimentary canal and digestive glands regarded as an integrated system responsible for the ingestion, digestion, and absorption of food

Reproductive System- The bodily system of gonads, associated ducts, and external genitals concerned with sexual reproduction

Renal System- The bodily system that consists of the kidneys and functions to regulate body activities

Skeletal System- The bodily system that consists of the bones, their associated cartilages, and the joints, and supports and protects the body, produces blood cells, and stores minerals

Immune System- The integrated body system of organs, tissues, cells, and cell products such as antibodies that differentiates self from nonself and neutralizes potentially pathogenic organisms or substances

Muscular System- The bodily system that is composed of skeletal, smooth, and cardiac muscle tissue and functions in movement of the body or of materials through the body, maintenance of posture, and heat production

Brain- The portion of the vertebrate central nervous system that is enclosed within the cranium, continuous with the spinal cord, and composed of gray matter and white matter. It is the primary center for the regulation and control of bodily activities, receiving and interpreting sensory impulses, and transmitting information to the muscles and body organs. It is also the seat of consciousness, thought, memory, and emotion

Spinal Cord- The thick, whitish cord of nerve tissue that extends from the medulla oblongata down through the spinal column and from which the spinal nerves branch off to various parts of the body

Earth and Space Science

Earth- The third planet from the sun, having a sidereal period of revolution about the sun of 365.26 days at a mean distance of approximately 149 million kilometers (92.96 million miles), an axial rotation period of 23 hours 56.07 minutes, an average radius of 6,378 kilometers (3,963 miles), and a mass of approximately 5.974×10^{24} kilograms (1.317×10^{25} pounds).

Sun- A star that is the basis of the solar system and that sustains life on Earth, being the source of heat and light. It has a mean distance from Earth of about 150 million kilometers (93 million miles) a diameter of approximately 1,390,000 kilometers (864,000 miles) and a mass about 330,000 times that of Earth

Internal Heat

Gravity-

    a. The natural force of attraction exerted by a celestial body, such as Earth, upon objects at or near its surface, tending to draw them toward the center of the body.

  b. The natural force of attraction between any two massive bodies, which is directly proportional to the product of their masses and inversely proportional to the square of the distance between them.

Waves-

  a. A disturbance traveling through a medium by which energy is transferred from one particle of the medium to another without causing any permanent displacement of the medium itself.

  b. A graphic representation of the variation of such a disturbance with time.

  c. A single cycle of such a disturbance.

Tectonics and Internal Earth Processes

Plate Tectonics- A theory that explains the global distribution of geological phenomena such as seismicity, volcanism, continental drift, and mountain building in terms of the formation, destruction, movement, and interaction of the earth's lithospheric plates

Trenches- A long, steep-sided valley on the ocean floor

Continental Drift- The movement, formation, or re-formation of continents described by the theory of plate tectonics

Fault- A fracture in the continuity of a rock formation caused by a shifting or dislodging of the earth's crust, in which adjacent surfaces are displaced relative to one another and parallel to the plane of fracture

A **seismic wave** is a wave that travels through the Earth, often as the result of an earthquake or explosion. Seismic waves are studied by seismologists, and measured by a seismograph.

Body waves travel through the interior of the Earth. They follow curved paths because of the varying density and composition of the Earth's interior. This effect is similar to the refraction of light waves. Body waves transmit the preliminary tremors of an earthquake but have little destructive effect. Body waves are divided into two types: primary (P) and secondary (S) waves.

Surface waves are analogous to water waves and travel over the Earth's surface. They travel more slowly than body waves. Because of their low frequency, they are more likely than body waves to stimulate resonance in buildings, and are therefore the most destructive type of seismic wave. There are two types of surface waves: Rayleigh waves and Love waves.

History of the Earth and its Life Forms

Fossil- A remnant or trace of an organism of a past geologic age, such as a skeleton or leaf imprint, embedded and preserved in the earth's crust

Paleontology- The study of the forms of life existing in prehistoric or geologic times, as represented by the fossils of plants, animals, and other organisms

Extinction- The act of extinguishing; no longer existing

Earth's Atmosphere and Hydrosphere

The water cycle is made up of a few main parts:

- **Evaporation**
- **Condensation**
- **Precipitation**
- **Collection**

Types of clouds:

Stratus Clouds- Stratus clouds are horizontal, layered clouds that stretch out across the sky like a blanket. Sometimes a layer of warm, moist air passes over a layer of cool air. Stratus clouds often form at the boundary where these layers meet. Where two such layers of air meet, the warm air is cooled. If the warm air is cooled below its dew point, the excess water vapor condenses to form a blanket

Cumulus Clouds- Cumulus clouds are puffy in appearance. They look like large cotton balls. Cumulus clouds usually form when warm, moist air is forced upward

Cirrus Clouds- Cirrus clouds are very wispy and feathery looking. They form only at high altitudes, about 7 km above the earth's surface. Cirrus clouds are composed of ice crystals and are so thin that sunlight can pass right through them

Climate- The meteorological conditions, including temperature, precipitation, and wind, that characteristically prevail in a particular region

Greenhouse effect- The phenomenon whereby the earth's atmosphere traps solar radiation, caused by the presence in the atmosphere of gases such as carbon dioxide, water vapor, and methane that allow incoming sunlight to pass through but absorb heat radiated back from the earth's surface.

Pollution- The act or process of polluting or the state of being polluted, especially the contamination of soil, water, or the atmosphere by the discharge of harmful substances.

Glacier- A huge mass of ice slowly flowing over a land mass, formed from compacted snow in an area where snow accumulation exceeds melting and sublimation.

Ice Age- A cold period marked by episodes of extensive glaciation alternating with episodes of relative warmth

Wave- A ridge or swell moving through or along the surface of a large body of water.

Tide- The periodic variation in the surface level of the oceans and of bays, gulfs, inlets, and estuaries, caused by gravitational attraction of the moon and sun.

Erosion- The group of natural processes, including weathering, dissolution, abrasion, corrosion, and transportation, by which material is worn away from the earth's surface.

Deposition- The act of depositing, especially the laying down of matter by a natural process.

Earth Materials and Surface Processes

Minerals- A naturally occurring, homogeneous inorganic solid substance having a definite chemical composition and characteristic crystalline structure, color, and hardness.

There are three types of rocks:

1. Igneous Rocks : Formed from the cooling of molten rock.

  A. Volcanic igneous rocks formed from molten rock that cooled quickly on or near the earth's surface.

B. Plutonic igneous rocks are the result of the slow cooling of molten rock far beneath the surface.

2. Sedimentary Rocks : Formed in layers as the result of moderate pressure on accumulated sediments.

3. Metamorphic Rocks : Formed from older "parent" rock (either igneous or sedimentary) under intense heat and/or pressure at considerable depths beneath the earth's surface.

There are four main layers that make up the earth:

1. Inner Core - A mass of iron with a temperature of about 7000 degrees F.

2. Outer Core - A mass of molten iron about 1,425 miles deep that surrounds the solid inner core.

3. Mantle - A rock layer about 1,750 miles thick that reaches about half the distance to the center of the earth.

4. Crust - A layer from 4-25 miles thick consisting of sand and rock.

Mechanical Weathering- Process by which rock is broken down into smaller and smaller fragments as result of energy developed by physical forces. Also known as disintegration.

Biological Weathering- The disintegration of rock and mineral due to the chemical and/or physical agents of an organism.

Chemical Weathering- Breakdown of rock and minerals into small sized particles through chemical decomposition.

Erosion- The group of natural processes, including weathering, dissolution, abrasion, corrosion, and transportation, by which material is worn away from the earth's surface.

Fossil Fuels- Solid, liquid, or gaseous fuels formed in the ground after millions of years by chemical and physical changes in plant and animal residues under high temperature and pressure.

Astronomy

Astronomy- The scientific study of matter in outer space, especially the positions, dimensions, distribution, motion, composition, energy, and evolution of celestial bodies and phenomena.

Star- A self-luminous celestial body consisting of a mass of gas held together by its own gravity in which the energy generated by nuclear reactions in the interior is balanced by the outflow of energy to the surface, and the inward-directed gravitational forces are balanced by the outward-directed gas and radiation pressures

Galaxies- Any of numerous large-scale aggregates of stars, gas, and dust that constitute the universe, containing an average of 100 billion (10^{11}) solar masses and ranging in diameter from 1,500 to 300,000 light-years

Solar System- A system of planets or other bodies orbiting another star

Planets- A nonluminous celestial body larger than an asteroid or comet, illuminated by light from a star, such as the sun, around which it revolves

Moon- The natural satellite of Earth, visible by reflection of sunlight and having a slightly elliptical orbit, approximately 356,000 kilometers (221,600 miles) distant at perigee and 406,997 kilometers (252,950 miles) at apogee.

Comet- A celestial body, observed only in that part of its orbit that is relatively close to the sun, having a head consisting of a solid nucleus surrounded by a nebulous coma up to 2.4 million kilometers (1.5 million miles) in diameter and an elongated curved vapor tail arising from the coma when sufficiently close to the sun.

Eclipses- The partial or complete obscuring, relative to a designated observer, of one celestial body by another.

Equinox- Either of the two times during a year when the sun crosses the celestial equator and when the length of day and night are approximately equal; the vernal equinox or the autumnal equinox.

Solstice- Either of two times of the year when the sun is at its greatest distance from the celestial equator.

Time Zone- Any of the 24 longitudinal divisions of Earth's surface in which a standard time is kept, the primary division being that bisected by the Greenwich meridian. Each zone is 15° of longitude in width, with local variations, and observes a clock time one hour earlier than the zone immediately to the east.

Asteroid Belt- The region of the solar system between the orbits of Mars and Jupiter, where most of the asteroids are found

Meteor- A bright trail or streak that appears in the sky when a meteoroid is heated to incandescence by friction with the earth's atmosphere.

Meteoroids- A solid body, moving in space, that is smaller than an asteroid and at least as large as a speck of dust.

Meteorites- A stony or metallic mass of matter that has fallen to the earth's surface from outer space.

Milky Way Galaxy- the galaxy containing the solar system; consists of millions of stars that can be seen as a diffuse band of light stretching across the night sky

Physical Science

Matter and Energy

Matter- Something that has mass and exists as a solid, liquid, gas, or plasma

Energy- The capacity for work or vigorous activity; vigor; power

Atom- A unit of matter, the smallest unit of an element, having all the characteristics of that element and consisting of a dense, central, positively charged nucleus surrounded by a system of electrons.

Molecule- The smallest particle of a substance that retains the chemical and physical properties of the substance and is composed of two or more atoms.

Ion- An atom or a group of atoms that has acquired a net electric charge by gaining or losing one or more electrons

States of Matter

- Solid
- Liquid
- Gas

Element- A substance composed of atoms having an identical number of protons in each nucleus.

Compound- A pure, macroscopically homogeneous substance consisting of atoms or ions of two or more different elements in definite proportions that cannot be separated by physical means.

Solution- A homogeneous mixture of two or more substances, which may be solids, liquids, gases, or a combination of these

Mixture- A composition of two or more substances that are not chemically combined with each other and are capable of being separated

Physical property- a property used to characterize physical objects

Chemical property- a property used to characterize materials in reactions that change their identity

Physical change- a change from one state (solid or liquid or gas) to another without a change in chemical composition

Chemical change- any process determined by the atomic and molecular composition and structure of the substances involved

Periodic Table- A tabular arrangement of the elements according to their atomic numbers so that elements with similar properties are in the same column.

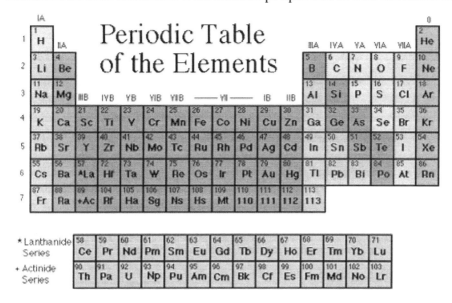

Nuclear Reaction- A reaction, as in fission, fusion, or radioactive decay, that alters the energy, composition, or structure of an atomic nucleus

Radioactive Decay- Spontaneous disintegration of a radionuclide accompanied by the emission of ionizing radiation in the form of alpha or beta particles or gamma rays

Carbon Dating- The determination of the approximate age of an ancient object, such as an archaeological specimen, by measuring the amount of carbon 14 it contains

Heat, Thermodynamics, and Thermochemistry

Heat- A form of energy associated with the motion of atoms or molecules and capable of being transmitted through solid and fluid media by conduction, through fluid media by convection, and through empty space by radiation

Temperature- A measure of the average kinetic energy of the particles in a sample of matter, expressed in terms of units or degrees designated on a standard scale

Celsius- Of or relating to a temperature scale that registers the freezing point of water as 0° and the boiling point as 100° under normal atmospheric pressure

Kelvin- A unit of absolute temperature equal to 1/273.16 of the absolute temperature of the triple point of water. One Kelvin degree is equal to one **Celsius degree**

Thermodynamics- Physics that deals with the relationships and conversions between heat and other forms of energy.

Vaporization- To convert or be converted into vapor

Sublimation- a change directly from the solid to the gaseous state without becoming liquid

Heat Capacity- The amount of heat required to raise the temperature of one mole or one gram of a substance by one degree Celsius without change of phase

Acid/Base Chemistry

Acid-

a. Any of a class of substances whose aqueous solutions are characterized by a sour taste, the ability to turn blue litmus red, and the ability to react with bases and certain metals to form salts.

b. A substance that yields hydrogen ions when dissolved in water.

c. A substance that can act as a proton donor.

d. A substance that can accept a pair of electrons to form a covalent bond.

Base-

a. Any of a class of compounds whose aqueous solutions are characterized by a bitter taste, a slippery feel, the ability to turn litmus blue, and the ability to react with acids to form salts.

b. A substance that yields hydroxyl ions when dissolved in water.

c. A substance that can act as a proton acceptor.

d. A substance that can donate a pair of electrons to form a covalent bond.

pH- p(otential of) H(ydrogen); the logarithm of the reciprocal of hydrogen-ion concentration in gram atoms per liter; used as a measure of the acidity or alkalinity of a solution on a scale of 0-14 (where 7 is neutral)

Scientific Procedures and Techniques

Be familiar with calculating time in terms of hours, minutes, and seconds. Also be familiar with the English Measurement system that includes: inches, feet, yards, miles, pint, quart, gallon, ounce, ton, and degrees Fahrenheit. Be familiar with the Metric system including: meters, liters, grams, kilometers, degrees Celsius. Know how to convert from one unit to another within the same system.

Collection- A group of objects or works to be seen, studied, or kept together

Analysis- The separation of an intellectual or material whole into its constituent parts for individual study

Interpretation- The act or process of interpreting

Presentation-

a. The act of presenting.

b. The state of being presented

Critical Analysis- an appraisal based on careful analytical evaluation

Be able to interpret and draw conclusions from different types of tables, graphs, and charts.

Independent Variable- A manipulated variable in an experiment or study whose presence or degree determines the change in the dependent variable

Dependent Variable- The observed variable in an experiment or study whose changes are determined by the presence or degree of one or more independent variables.

Mechanics & Dynamics

Physics- the science of matter and energy and their interactions

Newton's laws of motion

I. **Every object in a state of uniform motion tends to remain in that state of motion unless an external force is applied to it.**

Inertia- The tendency of a body to resist acceleration; the tendency of a body at rest to remain at rest or of a body in straight line motion to stay in motion in a straight line unless acted on by an outside force.

Galileo- Italian astronomer and mathematician; demonstrated that different weights descend at the same rate; perfected the refracting telescope that enabled him to make many discoveries

II. **The relationship between an object's mass m, its acceleration a, and the applied force F is $F = ma$. Acceleration and force are vectors (as indicated by their symbols being displayed in slant bold font); in this law the direction of the force vector is the same as the direction of the acceleration vector.**

Force- A vector quantity that tends to produce an acceleration of a body in the direction of its application

Acceleration- The rate of change of velocity with respect to time.

III. **For every action there is an equal and opposite reaction.**

Mass- A property of matter equal to the measure of an object's resistance to changes in either the speed or direction of its motion.

Weight- The force with which a body is attracted to Earth or another celestial body, equal to the product of the object's mass and the acceleration of gravity.

Friction- A force that resists the relative motion or tendency to such motion of two bodies in contact

Forms of Energy

- Chemical
- Electromagnetic
- Electrical
- Heat
- Kinetic
- Mechanical
- Nuclear
- Potential

Work- The transfer of energy from one physical system to another, especially the transfer of energy to a body by the application of a force that moves the body in the direction of the force.

Power- The rate at which work is done, expressed as the amount of work per unit time and commonly measured in units such as the watt and horsepower.

Momentum- The momentum of a particle is defined as the product of its mass times its velocity. It is a vector quantity.

Vector

 a. A quantity, such as velocity, completely specified by a magnitude and a direction

 b. A one-dimensional array

 c. An element of a vector space.

History and Nature of Science

Fact- Knowledge or information based on real occurrences

Hypothesis- A tentative explanation for an observation, phenomenon, or scientific problem that can be tested by further investigation

Theory- A set of statements or principles devised to explain a group of facts or phenomena, especially one that has been repeatedly tested or is widely accepted and can be used to make predictions about natural phenomena

Model- A schematic description of a system, theory, or phenomenon that accounts for its known or inferred properties and may be used for further study of its characteristics

Observation-

      a. The act of noting and recording something, such as a phenomenon, with instruments.

      b. The result or record of such notation

Conclusion- The result or outcome of an act or process

Scientific Method- The principles and empirical processes of discovery and demonstration considered characteristic of or necessary for scientific investigation, generally involving the observation of phenomena, the formulation of a hypothesis concerning the phenomena, experimentation to demonstrate the truth or falseness of the hypothesis, and a conclusion that validates or modifies the hypothesis.

Know these science process skills

- Observing
- Hypothesizing
- Ordering
- Categorizing
- Comparing
- Inferring
- Applying
- Communicating

Backtrack for Units

When faced with a problem that you don't know the formula for, simply solve for the units in the answer choices. The units in the answer choices are your key to understanding what mathematical relationship exists between the numbers given in the question.

Example: A 600 Hz sound wave has a velocity of 160 m/s. What is the wavelength of this sound wave?

Even if you do not know the formula for wavelengths, you can backtrack to get the answer by using the units in the answer choices. The answer choices are:

A. 0.17 m

B. 0.27 m

C. 0.35 m

D. 0.48 m

You know that Hz is equal to 1/s. To get an answer in m, when working with a m/s and a 1/s from the problem, you must divide the m/s by 1/s, which will leave an answer in meters or m. Therefore (160 m/s) / (600 1/s) = .27 m, making choice B correct.

Don't Fall for the Obvious

When in doubt of the answer, it is easy to go with what you are familiar with. If you recognize only one term in four answer choices, you may be inclined to guess at that term. Be careful though, and don't go with familiar answers simply because they are familiar.

Example: Changing the temperature of the solution to 373K would most likely result in:

A. boiling the solution

B. freezing the solution

C. dissolving the compound

D. saturating the solution

You know that 373K is the boiling point of pure water. Therefore choice A is familiar, because you have a mental link between the temperature 373K and the word "boiling". If you are unsure of the correct answer, you may decide upon choice A simply because of its familiarity. Don't be deceived though. Think through the other answer choices before making your final selection. Just because you have a mental link between two terms, doesn't make an answer choice correct.

Milk the Question

Some of the questions may throw you completely off. They might deal with a subject you have not been exposed to, or one that you haven't reviewed in years. While your lack of knowledge about the subject will be a hindrance, the question itself can give you many clues that will help you find the correct answer. Read the question carefully, and look for clues. Watch particularly for adjectives and nouns describing difficult terms or words that you don't recognize. Regardless of if you understand a word or not, replacing it with the synonyms used for it in the question may help you to understand what the questions are asking.

Example: A bacteriophage is a virus that infects bacteria....

While you may not know much information concerning the characteristics of a bacteriophage, the fifth word into the sentence told you that a bacteriophage is a virus. Whenever a question asks about a bacteriophage, you can mentally replace the word "bacteriophage" with the word "virus". Your more general knowledge of viruses will enable you to answer the question intelligibly.

Look carefully for these descriptive synonyms (nouns) and adjectives and use them to help you understand the difficult terms. Rather than wracking your mind about specific detail information concerning a difficult term in the question, use the more general description or synonym provided to make it easier for you.

Random Tips

- On fact questions that require choosing between numbers, don't guess the smallest or largest choice unless you're sure of the answer (remember- "sure" means you would bet $5 on it).
- For questions that you're not clear on the answer, use the process of elimination. Weed out the answer choices that you know are wrong before choosing an answer.

- Don't fall for "bizarre" choices, mentioning things that are not relevant to the passage. Also avoid answers that sound "smart." Again, if you're willing to bet $5, ignore the tips and go with your bet.

Vocabulary

Each multiple-choice question on the Vocabulary test presents a word in the context of a short phrase or sentence, and students select the answer that most nearly means the same as that word. Approximately equal numbers of nouns, verbs, and modifiers are tested. The target words represent general vocabulary content rather than the specialized vocabulary used in various subject-matter areas.

Nearly and Perfect Synonyms

You must determine which of five provided choices has the best similar definition as a certain word. Nearly similar may often be more correct, because the goal is to test your understanding of the nuances, or little differences, between words. A perfect match may not exist, so don't be concerned if your answer choice is not a complete synonym. Focus upon edging closer to the word. Eliminate the words that you know aren't correct first. Then narrow your search. Cross out the words that are the least similar to the main word until you are left with the one that is the most similar.

Prefixes

Take advantage of every clue that the word might include. Prefixes and suffixes can be a huge help. Usually they allow you to determine a basic meaning. Pre- means before, post- means after, pro – is positive, de- is negative. From these prefixes and suffixes, you can get an idea of the general meaning of the word and look for its opposite. Beware though of any traps. Just because con is the opposite of pro, doesn't necessarily mean congress is the opposite of progress! A list of the most common prefixes and suffixes is included in the appendix.

Positive vs. Negative

Many words can be easily determined to be a positive word or a negative word. Words such as despicable, gruesome, and bleak are all negative. Words such as ecstatic, praiseworthy, and magnificent are all positive. You will be surprised at how many words can be considered as either positive or negative. Once that is determined, you can quickly eliminate any other words with an opposite meaning and focus on those that have the other characteristic, whether positive or negative.

Word Strength

Part of the challenge is determining the most nearly similar word. This is particularly true when two words seem to be similar. When analyzing a word, determine how strong it is. For example, stupendous and good are both positive words. However, stupendous is a much stronger positive adjective than good. Also, towering or gigantic are stronger words than tall or large. Search for an answer choice that is similar and also has the same strength. If the main word is weak, look for similar words that are also weak. If the main word is strong, look for similar words that are also strong.

Type and Topic

Another key is what type of word is the main word. If the main word is an adjective describing height, then look for the answer to be an adjective describing height as well. Match both the type and topic of the main word. The type refers the parts of speech, whether the word is an adjective, adverb, or verb. The topic refers to what the definition of the word includes, such as sizes or fashion styles.

Form a Sentence

Many words seem more natural in a sentence. *Specious* reasoning, *irresistible* force, and *uncanny* resemblance are just a few of the word combinations that usually go together. When faced with an uncommon word that you barely understand, try to put the word in a sentence that makes sense. It will help you to understand the word's meaning and make it easier to determine its opposite. Once you have a good descriptive sentence that utilizes the main word properly, plug in the answer choices and see if the sentence still has the same meaning with each answer choice. The answer choice that maintains the meaning of the sentence is correct!

Use Replacements

Using a sentence is a great help because it puts the word into a proper perspective. Read the provided sentence with the underlined word. Then read the sentence again and again, each time replacing the underlined word with one of the answer choices. The correct answer should "sound" right and fit.

Example: The desert landscape was **desolate**.

    A. cheerful

    B. creepy

    C. excited

    D. forlorn

After reading the example sentence, begin replacing "desolate" with each of the answer choices. Does "the desert landscape was cheerful, creepy, excited, or forlorn" sound right? Deserts are typically hot, empty, and rugged environments, probably not cheerful, or excited. While creepy might sound right, that word would certainly be more appropriate for a haunted house. But "the desert landscape was forlorn" has a certain ring to it and would be correct.

Eliminate Similar Choices

If you don't know the word, don't worry. Look at the answer choices and just use them. Remember that three of the answer choices will always be wrong. If you can find a common relationship between any three answer choices, then you know they are wrong. Find the answer choice that does not have a common relationship to the other answer choices and it will be the correct answer.

Example: **Laconic** most nearly means

    A. wordy

    B. talkative

    C. expressive

D. quiet

In this example the first three choices are all similar. Even if you don't know that laconic means the same as quiet, you know that "quiet" must be correct, because the other three choices were all virtually the same. They were all the same, so they must all be wrong. The one that is different must be correct. So, don't worry if you don't know a word. Focus on the answer choices that you do understand and see if you can identify similarities. Even identifying two words that are similar will allow you to eliminate those two answer choices, for they are both wrong, because they are either both right or both wrong (they're similar, remember), so since they can't both be right, they both must be wrong.

The Trap of Familiarity

Don't choose a word just because you recognize it. On difficult questions, you may only recognize one or two words. ITBS doesn't put "make-believe" words on the test, so don't think that just because you only recognize one word means that word must be correct. If you don't recognize four words, then focus on the one that you do recognize. Is it correct? Try your best to determine if it fits the sentence. If it does, that is great, but if it doesn't, eliminate it. Each word you eliminate increases your chances of getting the question correct.

Read Carefully

Be sure to read all of the choices. You may find an answer choice that seems right at first, but continue reading and you may find a better choice.

Difficult words are usually synonyms or antonyms (opposites). Whenever you have extremely difficult words that you don't understand, look at the answer choices. Try and identify whether two or more of the answer choices are either synonyms or antonyms. Remember that if you can find two words that have the same relationship (for example, two answer choices are synonyms) then you can eliminate them both.

Spelling, Capitalization, Punctuation, Usage & Expression

Simplicity is Bliss
Simplicity cannot be overstated.

Beware of added phrases that don't add anything of meaning, such as "to be" or "as to them". Often these added phrases will occur just before a colon, which may come before a list of items. However, the colon does not need a lengthy introduction. The phrases "of which [...] are" in the below examples are wordy and unnecessary. They should be removed and the colon placed directly after the words "sport" and "following".

Example 1: There are many advantages to running as a sport, of which the top advantages are:

Example 2: The school supplies necessary were the following, of which a few are:

Parallelism
Often clues to the best answer are given within the text, if you know where to look for them. The correct answer will always be parallel in grammar type, punctuation, format, and tense as the rest of the sentence.

Grammar Type
If a series of nouns is given, then make sure your choice is a noun. If those nouns are plural, then ensure that your choice is plural.

Example: schools, politics, and governments

If a series of verbs is given, then make sure your choice is a verb.

Example: eat, sleep, and drink

If a series of infinitives is given, then make sure your choice is an infinitive.

Example: to trust, to honor, and to obey

If a series of phrases is given, then make sure your choice is a similar phrase.

Example: of controlling, of policing, and of maintaining

Punctuation

If a section of text has an opening dash, parentheses, or comma at the beginning of a phrase, then you can be sure there should be a matching closing dash, parentheses, or comma at the end of the phrase. If items in a series all have commas between them, then any additional items in that series will also gain commas. Do not alternate punctuation. If a dash is at the beginning of a statement, then do not put a parenthesis at the ending of the statement.

Tense

Items in a series will also have the same tense.

If past tense is being used for the other items in the series, then maintain the same past tense for your response.

Example: sailed, flew, and raced

If present participle tense is being used for the other items in the series, then maintain the same present participle tense for your response.

Example: sailing, flying, and racing

In order to test the tense of a verb, you can put it into a sentence that includes yourself. I sailed the boat. I flew the plane. I raced the car. These all fit into similar sentence structures and are in fact the same tense.

Added phrases

Any sentence or phrase added to a paragraph must maintain the same train of thought. This is particularly true when the word "and" is used. The word "and" joins two comments of like nature.

Example: These men were tough. They were accustomed to a hard life, and could watch a man die without blinking.

If an added phrase does not maintain a consistent train of thought, it will be set out with a word such as "but", "however", or "although". The new phrase would then be inconsistent to the train of thought and would offer a contrast.

Example: These men were tough. They were accustomed to a hard life, but to watch a man die would cause them to faint.

A tough man accustomed to a hard life is not expected to faint. Therefore the statements are contrasting and must have a contrasting transitional word, such as "but."

Word Confusion

Contractions

All contractions, such as they're, it's, and who's are actually two words joined together by the use of an apostrophe to replace a missing letter or letters. Whenever a contraction is encountered, it can be broken down into the two distinct words that make it up.

Example: I wouldn't eat in the cafeteria. = I would not eat in the cafeteria.

The apostrophe in the contraction is always located where the missing letter or letters should be. In the examples below, the apostrophe replaces the "o" in the word "not". The contraction "doesn't" actually stands for the two words "does not".

Incorrect Example: He does'nt live here.
Correct Example: He doesn't live here.

Whenever there is a contraction in an answer choice, it can always be replaced by the two words that make the contraction up. If necessary, scratch through the contractions in the choices, and replace them with the two words that make up the contraction. Otherwise the choices may be confusing. Alternatively, while reading the answer choices to yourself, instead of reading the contractions as a contraction, read them as the two separate words that make them up. Some contractions are especially confusing.

Its/It's

"It's" is actually a contraction for the two words "it is". Never confuse "it's" for the possessive pronoun "its". "It's" should only be used when the two words "it is" would make sense as a replacement. Use "its" in all other cases.

Example 1: It's going to rain later today. = It is going to rain later today.
Example 2: The dog chewed through its rope and ran away.

They're/Their/There

"They're" is actually a contraction for "they are", and those two words should always be used to replace "they're" when it is encountered.

Example: They're going to the movie with us. = They are going to the movie with us.

"Their" is an adjective used to show ownership.

Example 1: Their car is a red convertible.

Example 2: The students from each school sat in their own stands.

"There" should be used in all other cases.

Example 1: There exists an answer to every question.

Example 2: The man was over there.

Who's/Whose

Who's is actually a contraction for "who is", and those two words should always be used to replace who's when it is encountered.

Example: Who's going with me? = Who is going with me?

Whose would be used in all other cases, where "who is" does not fit.

Example: Whose car is this?

Their/His

"Their" is a plural possessive pronoun, referring to multiple people or objects.

Example: The men went to their cars.

"His" is a singular possessive, referring to an individual person or object.

Example: The man went to his car.

Which/That/Who

"Which" should be used to refer to things only.

John's dog, which was called Max, is large and fierce.

"That" may be used to refer to either persons or things.

Is this the only book that Louis L'Amour wrote?

Is Louis L'Amour the author that [or who] wrote Western novels?

"Who" should be used to refer to persons only.

Mozart was the composer who [or that] wrote those operas.

Who/Whom or Whoever/Whomever

Who/whom will be encountered in two forms, as an interrogative pronoun in a question, or as a relative pronoun not in a question.

1. Interrogative pronoun in a question. If the answer to the question would include the pronouns he, she, we, or they, then "who" is correct.

Example: Who threw the ball? He threw the ball.

If the answer to the question would include the pronouns him, her, us, or them, then "whom" is correct.

Example: With whom did you play baseball? I played baseball with him.

2. Relative pronoun NOT in a question.

If who/whom is followed by a verb, typically use "who".

Example: Peter Jackson was an obscure director who became a celebrity overnight.

If who/whom is followed by a noun, typically use "whom".

Example: Bob, whom we follow throughout his career, rose swiftly up the ladder of success.

However, beware of the insertion of phrases or expressions immediately following the use of who/whom. Sometimes, the phrase can be skipped without the sentence losing its meaning.

Example: This is the woman who, we believe, will win the race.

To determine the proper selection of who/whom, skip the phrase "we believe".

Thus, "who" would come before "will win", a verb, making the choice of "who" correct.

In other cases, the sentence should be rephrased in order to make the right decision.

Example: I can't remember who the author of "War and Peace" is.

To determine the proper selection of who/whom, rephrase the sentence to state, "I can't remember who is the author of 'War and Peace'."

Correct pronoun usage in combinations

To determine the correct pronoun form in a compound subject, try each subject separately with the verb, adapting the form as necessary. Your ear will tell you which form is correct.

Example: Bob and (I, me) will be going.

Restate the sentence twice, using each subject individually. Bob will be going. I will be going.

"Me will be going" does not make sense.

When a pronoun is used with a noun immediately following (as in "we boys"), say the sentence without the added noun. Your ear will tell you the correct pronoun form.

Example: (We/Us) boys played football last year.

Restate the sentence twice, without the noun. We played football last year. Us played football last year. Clearly "We played football last year" makes more sense.

Commas

Flow

Commas break the flow of text. To test whether they are necessary, while reading the text to yourself, pause for a moment at each comma. If the pauses seem natural, then the commas are correct. If they are not, then the commas are not correct.

Nonessential clauses and phrases

A comma should be used to set off nonessential clauses and nonessential participial phrases from the rest of the sentence. To determine if a clause is essential, remove it from the sentence. If the removal of the clause would alter the meaning of the sentence, then it is essential. Otherwise, it is nonessential.

Example: John Smith, who was a disciple of Andrew Collins, was a noted archeologist.

In the example above, the sentence describes John Smith's fame in archeology. The fact that he was a disciple of Andrew Collins is not necessary to that meaning. Therefore, separating it from the rest of the sentence with commas, is correct.

Do not use a comma if the clause or phrase is essential to the meaning of the sentence.

Example: Anyone who appreciates obscure French poetry will enjoy reading the book.

If the phrase "who appreciates obscure French poetry" is removed, the sentence would indicate that anyone would enjoy reading the book, not just those with an appreciation for obscure French poetry. However, the sentence implies that the book's enjoyment may not be for everyone, so the phrase is essential.

Another perhaps easier way to determine if the clause is essential is to see if it has a comma at its beginning or end. Consistent, parallel punctuation must be used, and so if you can determine a comma exists at one side of the clause, then you can be certain that a comma should exist on the opposite side.

Subjects and verbs

Subjects and verbs must not be separated by commas. However, a pair of commas setting off a nonessential phrase is allowed.

Example: The office, which closed today for the festival, was open on Thursday. "Was" is the verb, while "office" is the subject. The comma pair between them sets off a nonessential phrase, "which is allowed". A single comma between them would not be allowed.
If you are trying to find the subject, first find the verb and use it to fill in the blank in the following sentence. Who or what ____?

Example: The boy on the bicycle raced down the hill.
The verb is "raced". If you can find "raced" and identify it as the verb, ask yourself, "Who or what raced down the hill?" The answer to that question is the subject, in this case "boy".

Independent clauses

Use a comma before the words and, but, or, nor, for, yet when they join independent clauses. To determine if two clauses are independent, remove the word that joins them. If the two clauses are capable of being their own sentence by themselves, then they are independent and need a comma between them.

Example: He ran down the street, and then he ran over the bridge.

He ran down the street. Then he ran over the bridge. These are both clauses capable of being their own sentence. Therefore a comma must be used along with the word "and" to join the two clauses together.

If one or more of the clauses would be a fragment if left alone, then it must be joined to another clause and does not need a comma between them.

Example: He ran down the street and over the bridge.

He ran down the street. Over the bridge. "Over the bridge" is a sentence fragment and is not capable of existing on its own. No comma is necessary to join it with "He ran down the street".

Note that this does not cover the use of "and" when separating items in a series, such as "red, white, and blue". In these cases a comma is not always necessary between the last two items in the series, but in general it is best to use one.

Parenthetical expressions

Commas should separate parenthetical expressions such as the following: after all, by the way, for example, in fact, on the other hand.

Example: By the way, she is in my biology class.

If the parenthetical expression is in the middle of the sentence, a comma would be both before and after it.

Example: She is, after all, in my biology class.

However, these expressions are not always used parenthetically. In these cases, commas are not used. To determine if an expression is parenthetical, see if it would need a pause if you were reading the text. If it does, then it is parenthetical and needs commas.

Example: You can tell by the way she plays the violin that she enjoys its music. No pause is necessary in reading that example sentence. Therefore the phrase "by the way" does not need commas around it.

Sentence beginnings

Use a comma after words such as so, well, yes, no, and why when they begin a sentence.

Example 1: So, you were there when they visited.

Example 2: Well, I really haven't thought about it.

Example 3: Yes, I heard your question.

Example 4: No, I don't think I'll go to the movie.

Example 5: Why, I can't imagine where I left my keys.

Hyphens

Hyphenate a compound adjective that is directly before the noun it describes.

Example 1: He was the best-known kid in the school.

Example 2: The shot came from that grass-covered hill.

Example 3: The well-drained fields were dry soon after the rain.

Semicolons

Period replacement

A semicolon is often described as either a weak period or strong comma. Semicolons should separate independent clauses that could stand alone as separate sentences. To test where a semicolon should go, replace it with a period in your mind. If the two independent clauses would seem normal with the period, then the semicolon is in the right place.

Example: The rain had finally stopped; a few rays of sunshine were pushing their way through the clouds.

The rain had finally stopped. A few rays of sunshine were pushing their way through the clouds. These two sentences can exist independently with a period between them. Because they are also closely related in thought, a semicolon is a good choice to combine them.

Related/Unrelated

A semicolon should only join clauses that are closely related in thought.

Example: The lasagna is delicious; I'll have another piece.

In this example, the two clauses are closely related in thought; a semicolon should join them.

Do not use a semicolon if the clauses are unrelated in thought.

Example: For Steve, oil painting was a difficult medium to master. He had enjoyed taking photographs when he was younger.

In this example, the two sentences would be unrelated clauses, so a semicolon should not join them.

Comparative methods of joining clauses

Use a semicolon between independent clauses not joined by "and, but, for, or, nor, yet, so, since, therefore". Semicolons should rarely be next to these words, but is rather used in place of a comma and these words.

Example 1: He had the gun; it hung from a holster at his side.

In the example above, no "and" or comma is necessary.

Example 2: He had the gun, and it hung from a holster at his side.

In the example above, the comma combined with the word "and" help to join the two independent clauses.

Transitions

When a semicolon is next to a transition word, such as "however", it comes before the word.

Example: The man in the red shirt stood next to her; however, he did not know her name.

If these two clauses were separated with a period, the period would go before the word "however" creating the following two sentences: The man in the red shirt stood next to her. However, he did not know her name. The semicolon can function as a weak period and join the two clauses by replacing the period.

Items in a series

Semicolons are used to separate 3 or more items in a series that have a comma internally.

Example: The club president appointed the following to chair the various committees: John Smith, planning; Jessica Graham, membership; Paul Randolph, financial; and Jerry Short, legal.

Parentheses

Years

Parentheses should be used around years.

Example: The presidency of Franklin Delano Roosevelt (1932-1945) was the longest one in American history.

Nonessential information

Parentheses can be used around information that is added to a sentence but is not essential. Commas or dashes could also be used around these nonessential phrases.

Example: George Eliot (whose real name was Mary Ann Evans) wrote poems and several well-known novels.

Colon

Items in a series

A colon should precede a list of items in which you could logically insert the word "namely" after it.

Example: The syllabus stated that each student would need the following: a sketch pad, a set of paint brushes, an easel, a pencil, and a box of crayons.

If the word namely were inserted, the example sentence would read, "The syllabus stated that each student would need the following: "namely" a sketch pad, a set of paint brushes, an easel, a pencil, and a box of crayons." Because the sentence still flows with the word "namely" inserted, a colon is necessary.

When the list immediately follows a verb or preposition, do not use a colon.

Example 1: The emergency kit included safety flares, jumper cables, and a flashlight.

Example 2: Each student taking the test was provided with two sharpened pencils, paper, a calculator, and a ruler.

Note that the insertion of the word "namely" would be awkward in the above two examples.

Independent clauses

Use a colon between independent clauses when the second clause explains or restates the idea of the first.

Example: Benjamin Franklin had many talents: he was an inventor, a writer, a politician, and a philosopher.

Apostrophes

If the noun is plural and ends in an "s", the possessive apostrophe would come after the word, without the addition of another "s".

Example: The students' hats were wet from the rain.

In the example above, there are plural or many students, all of whom have wet hats.

If the noun is plural and does not end in an "s", the possessive apostrophe would come after the word, with the addition of an "s".

Example: The mice's feet were wet from the rain.

If the noun is singular, the possessive apostrophe is followed by an "s".

Example: The student's hat was wet from the rain.

In the example above, there is only one student, whose hat is wet.

Social Studies

Geography

Longitude- Angular distance on the earth's surface, measured east or west from the prime meridian at Greenwich, England, to the meridian passing through a position, expressed in degrees (or hours), minutes, and seconds

Latitude- The angular distance north or south of the earth's equator, measured in degrees along a meridian, as on a map or globe

Equator- The imaginary great circle around the earth's surface, equidistant from the poles and perpendicular to the earth's axis of rotation. It divides the earth into the Northern Hemisphere and the Southern Hemisphere

International Dateline- An imaginary line on the surface of the earth following (approximately) the 180th meridian

Know the seven continents and their locations

Africa, Asia, Europe, Antarctica, North America, South America, and Australia

Know the four oceans

Indian Ocean, Pacific Ocean, Atlantic Ocean, and Artic Ocean

Know how to read a map and map legend. Be able to identify and interpret different kinds of maps. Know the kids of geographic features that make up the earth.

Weather- The state of the atmosphere at a given time and place, with respect to variables such as temperature, moisture, wind velocity, and barometric pressure

Climate- The meteorological conditions, including temperature, precipitation, and wind, that characteristically prevail in a particular region

Know how floods, droughts, earthquakes, erosion and snowstorms affect the Earth

Understand factors that affect settlement patterns and immigration. Know why some areas are sparsely populated while some areas are densely populated. Know immigration patterns and trends in the United States in the 19th and 20th centuries. Know the trends in the ethnic composition of the United States population.

International Organizations:

European Union (EU)- An economic and political union established in 1993 after the ratification of the Maastricht Treaty by members of the European Community, which forms its core. In establishing the European Union, the treaty expanded the political scope of the European Community, especially in the area of foreign and security policy, and provided for the creation of a central European bank and the adoption of a common currency by the end of the 20th century

World Trade Organization (WTO)- Administers the rules governing trade between its 144 Members. These rules help producers, exporters, and importers conduct their business, and ensure that trade flows as smoothly and predictably as possible. These rules also respect the right of governments to pursue broader goals such as sustainable development, the protection of human, animal or plant health, and the provision of public services

United Nations (UN)- An international organization composed of most of the countries of the world. It was founded in 1945 to promote peace, security, and economic development

North Atlantic Treaty Organization (NATO)- An international organization created in 1949 by the North Atlantic Treaty for purposes of collective security

Organization of Petroleum Exporting Countries (**OPEC**) – An organization of countries formed in 1961 to agree on a common policy for the sale of petroleum

Be able to comprehend the impact of the environment on human systems such as main essentials, transportation and recreation, and economic and industrial systems. Also know the effects of human initiated changes on the environment such

- 83 -

as pollution, new construction, waste, global warming, ozone depletion. Understand what natural resources are and why they are important. Know what the ecosystem is and why it is important.

World History

Prehistoric and early Civilization

Paleolithic- of or relating to the cultural period of the Stone Age beginning with the earliest chipped stone tools, about 750,000 years ago, until the beginning of the Mesolithic Age, about 15,000 years ago. Also known as Old Stone Age.

Neolithic- of or relating to the cultural period of the Stone Age beginning around 10,000 B.C. in the Middle East and later elsewhere, characterized by the development of agriculture and the making of polished stone implements. Also known as New Stone Age

Know major characteristics of the following civilizations:

Mesopotamia (c. 3500-c. 2350 B.C.)
Indus River Valley (c. 2500- c. 1750 B.C.)
Early China (c. 1500-c. 771 B.C.)
Olmec society in Mesoamerica (c. 1200-c.400 B.C.)

Classic Civilizations

List the influences of geography on the civilization

Ancient Egypt (C. 2700-c. 1090 B.C.)

- Religious rulership
- Pyramids and the Valley of /kings
- Hieroglyphics and the Rosetta Stone

Greece (c. 2000-c. 300 B.C.)

- Mythology
- Social structure and the concepts of citizenship
- commerce, the city-state, and colonies
- Alexander the Great- king of Macedon; conqueror of Greece and Egypt and Persia; founder of Alexandria
- Athens

- Sparta

Rome (c. 700 B.C.- 500 A.D.)

- Mythology
- Military dominance
- Stages of government
- Origin and Spread of Christianity
- Constantinople
- Reason for the fall of the empire

Non-European Civilizations

India

- Caste system
- Hinduism- diverse body of religion, philosophy, and cultural practice native to and predominant in India, characterized by a belief in reincarnation and a supreme being of many forms and natures, by the view that opposing theories are aspects of one eternal truth, and by a desire for liberation from earthly evils
- Muslim conquest

Islam- a monotheistic religion characterized by the acceptance of the doctrine of submission to God and to Muhammad as the chief and last prophet of God

China

- Buddhism- the teaching of Buddha that life is permeated with suffering caused by desire, that suffering ceases when desire ceases, and that enlightenment obtained through right conduct, wisdom, and meditation releases one from desire, suffering, and rebirth
- Confucianism- of, relating to, or characteristic of Confucius, his teachings, or his followers
- Taoism- a principal philosophy and system of religion of China based on the teachings of Lao-tzu in the sixth century B.C. and on subsequent revelations. It advocates preserving and restoring the Tao in the body and the cosmos
- Construction of the Great Wall

Japan

- Feudalism- a political and economic system based on the holding of all land in fief or fee and the resulting relation of lord to vassal and characterized by homage, legal and military service of tenants, and forfeiture
- Shinotism- religion native to Japan, characterized by veneration of nature spirits and ancestors and by a lack of formal dogma
- Buddhism- see above
- Samurai, emperors, shoguns

Central and South America

- Mayas- a member of a Mesoamerican Indian people inhabiting southeast Mexico, Guatemala, and Belize, whose civilization reached its height around A.D. 300-900. The Maya are noted for their architecture and city planning, their mathematics and calendar, and their hieroglyphic writing system
- Aztecs- a member of a people of central Mexico whose civilization was at its height at the time of the Spanish conquest in the early 16th century
- Incas- a member of the group of Quechuan peoples of highland Peru who established an empire from northern Ecuador to central Chile before the Spanish conquest

Sub-Saharan African

- Trading empires
- Forest kingdoms

Rise and Expansion of Europe

- Feudalism- a political and economic system of Europe from the 9th to about the 15th century, based on the holding of all land in fief or fee and the resulting relation of lord to vassal and characterized by homage, legal and military service of tenants, and forfeiture
- The Black Death- the epidemic form of bubonic plague experienced during the Middle Ages when it killed nearly half the people of western Europe
- French Revolution- the revolution in France against the Bourbons; 1789-1799
- Napoleon Bonaparte- Emperor of the French (1804-1814). A brilliant military strategist, he deposed the French Directory (1799) and proclaimed himself first consul and, later, emperor (1804). His military and political might gripped Continental Europe but failed to encompass Great Britain. After a disastrous winter campaign in Russia (1812), he was forced to abdicate (1814). Having been exiled to the island of Elba, he escaped, briefly regained power, and was ultimately defeated at Waterloo (1815) and exiled for life to the island of St. Helena. His codification of laws, the Napoleonic Code, still forms the basis of French civil law

- Industrial Revolution- The complex of radical socioeconomic changes, such as the ones that took place in England in the late 18th century, that are brought about when extensive mechanization of production systems results in a shift from home-based hand manufacturing to large-scale factory production
- Know the European colonies in Africa and Asia at the end of the 19th century
- Enlightenment

  - Locke
  - Rousseau
  - Jefferson

- Scientific Revolution

  - Newton- English mathematician and scientist who invented differential calculus and formulated the theory of universal gravitation, a theory about the nature of light, and three laws of motion. His treatise on gravitation, presented in *Principia Mathematica* (1687), was supposedly inspired by the sight of a falling apple
  - Galileo- Italian astronomer and mathematician; demonstrated that different weights descend at the same rate; perfected the refracting telescope that enabled him to make many discoveries (1564-1642)
  - Copernicus- Polish astronomer who advanced the theory that Earth and the other planets revolve around the sun, disrupting the Ptolemaic system of astronomy

- Reformation- A 16th-century movement in Western Europe that aimed at reforming some doctrines and practices of the Roman Catholic Church and resulted in the establishment of the Protestant churches

  - John Calvin
  - Martin Luther

- Renaissance- The humanistic revival of classical art, architecture, literature, and learning that originated in Italy in the 14th century and later spread throughout Europe

  - Da Vinci
  - Michelangelo
  - Machiavelli

- Know the voyages and conquest of the following:

- o Marco Polo- Venetian traveler who explored Asia from 1271 to 1295. His *Travels of Marco Polo* was the only account of the Far East available to Europeans until the 17th century

- o Christopher Columbus- Italian explorer in the service of Spain who determined that the earth was round and attempted to reach Asia by sailing west from Europe, thereby discovering America (1492). He made three subsequent voyages to the Caribbean in his quest for a sea route to China

- o Ferdinand Magellan- Portuguese navigator. While trying to find a western route to the Moluccas (1519), Magellan and his expedition were blown by storms into the strait that now bears his name (1520). He named and sailed across the Pacific Ocean, reaching the Marianas and the Philippines (1521), where he was killed fighting for a friendly native king. One of his ships returned to Spain (1522), thereby completing the first circumnavigation of the globe

- o Vasco da Gama- Portuguese explorer and colonial administrator. The first European to sail to India (1497-1498), he opened the rich lands of the East to Portuguese trade and colonization

20th Century Developments and Transformation

World War 1- a war between the allies (Russia, France, British Empire, Italy, United States, Japan, Rumania, Serbia, Belgium, Greece, Portugal, Montenegro) and the central powers (Germany, Austria-Hungary, Turkey, Bulgaria) from 1914 to 1918

Russian Revolution- the coup d'etat by the Bolsheviks under Lenin in November 1917 that led to a period of civil war which ended in victory for the Bolsheviks in 1922

Mexican Revolution- a Republic in southern North America; became independent from Spain in 1810

Chinese Revolution- the republican revolution against the Manchu dynasty in China; 1911-1912

Communism- A system of government in which the state plans and controls the economy and a single, often authoritarian party holds power, claiming to make progress toward a higher social order in which all goods are equally shared by the people

World War 2- a war between the Allies (Australia, Belgium, Bolivia, Brazil, Canada, China, Colombia, Costa Rica, Cuba, Czechoslovakia, Dominican Republic, El Salvador, Ethiopia, France, Greece, Guatemala, Haiti, Honduras, India, Iran, Iraq, Luxembourg, Mexico, Netherlands, New Zealand, Nicaragua, Norway, Panama, Philippines, Poland, South Africa, United Kingdom, United States, USSR, Yugoslavia) and the Axis (Albania, Bulgaria, Finland, Germany, Hungary, Italy, Japan, Rumania, Slovakia, Thailand) from 1939 to 1945

Holocaust- The genocide of European Jews and others by the Nazis during World War II: "Israel emerged from the Holocaust and is defined in relation to that catastrophe

Cold War- (c. 1945-1990) was the conflict between the two groups, loosely categorized as the *West* (the United States and its North Atlantic Treaty Organization (NATO) allies) and the *East* (the Soviet Union and its Warsaw Pact allies - loosely described as the Eastern Bloc). A full-scale "east versus west" war never actually broke out, hence the metaphor of a "cold" war with a predilection for quashing armed conflicts to prevent a "hot" and escalating shooting war whenever possible. Indeed, a good show was made on both sides that the conflict was primarily about economic, philosophic, cultural, social, and political ideology. The West criticized the East as embodying undemocratic totalitarianism and communist dictatorship while the East criticized the West as promoting bourgeois capitalism and imperialism. The attitude of both sides towards the other was summed up in the phrases used against each other; the East accused the West of promoting "middle class capitalism and imperialism that sidelined workers" while the West in the 1980s called the East the "evil empire" intent on subverting democracy for communist ideology

Lenin- Russian founder of the Bolsheviks, leader of the Russian Revolution (1917), and first head of the USSR (1917-1924). As a communist theoretician Lenin held that workers could not develop a revolutionary consciousness without the guidance of a vanguard party and that imperialism was a particular stage of capitalist development

Stalin- Soviet politician. The successor of Lenin, he was general secretary of the Communist Party (1922-1953) and premier (1941-1953) of the USSR. His rule was marked by the exile of Trotsky (1929), a purge of the government and military, the forced collectivization of agriculture, a policy of industrialization, and a victorious but devastating role for the Soviets in World War II

Mao Zedong- Chinese Communist leader and theorist. A founder of the Chinese Communist Party (1921), he led the Long March (1934-1935) and proclaimed the People's Republic of China in 1949. As party chairman and the country's first head of state (1949-1959) he initiated the Great Leap Forward and the founding of communes. He continued as party chairman after 1959 and was a leading figure in the Cultural Revolution (1966-1969). In the 1970s he consolidated his political power and established ties with the West

Mohandas Gandhi- Indian nationalist and spiritual leader who developed the practice of nonviolent disobedience that forced Great Britain to grant independence to India (1947). He was assassinated by a Hindu fanatic

Nelson Mandela- South African president (1994-1999) and Black political leader imprisoned for nearly 30 years for his anti-apartheid activities. Released in 1990, he led the African National Congress in negotiating an end to apartheid. In 1993 he shared the Nobel Peace Prize.

Post-Second World War decolinization in Africa and Asia and increased democracy in Europe, including:

- o India and Pakistan in 1947
- o Sub-Saharan nations in 1960s
- o Kenya, Angola, Mozabambique in the 1960's and 19+70's
- o Nations in Eastern Europe, the Balkans, and the former Soviet Union in the 1980's and 1990's
- o Fall of the Berlin Wall 1989

Know the rise of global culture and the rise of a global economy.

United States History
European Exploration and Colonization

Inuit- A member of a group of Eskimoan peoples inhabiting the Arctic from northern Alaska eastward to eastern Greenland, particularly those of Canada

Anasazi- A Native American culture flourishing in southern Colorado and Utah and northern New Mexico and Arizona from about A.D. 100, whose descendants are considered to include the present-day Pueblo people. Anasazi culture includes an early Basket Maker phase and a later Pueblo phase marked by the construction of cliff dwellings and by expert artisanship in weaving and pottery

Northwest Indians- A Native American people inhabiting parts of coastal British Columbia and northern Vancouver Island

Mound Builders- the tribe, or tribes, of North American aborigines who built, in former times, extensive mounds of earth, esp. in the valleys of the Mississippi and Ohio Rivers. Formerly they were supposed to have preceded the Indians, but later investigations go to show that they were, in general, identical with the tribes that occupied the country when discovered by Europeans

Iroquois- A Native American confederacy inhabiting New York State and originally composed of the Mohawk, Oneida, Onondaga, Cayuga, and Seneca peoples, known as the Five Nations. After 1722 the confederacy was joined by the Tuscaroras to form the Six Nations

Know and understand the interactions between the Native Americans and the Europeans. Understand colonial culture from different perspectives.

The American Revolution and the founding of the Nation

American Revolution- the revolution of the American colonies against Great Britain; 1775-1783

Declaration of Independence- the document recording the proclamation of the second Continental Congress (4 July 1776) asserting the independence of the colonies from Great Britain

Articles of Confederation- a written agreement ratified in 1781 by the thirteen original states; it provided a legal symbol of their union by gave the central government no coercive power over the states or their citizens

John Adams- The first Vice President (1789-1797) and second President (1797-1801) of the United States. He was a major figure during the American Revolution, the drafting of the Declaration of Independence, and the shaping of the Constitution

Thomas Jefferson- The third President of the United States (1801-1809). A member of the second Continental Congress, he drafted the Declaration of Independence (1776). His presidency was marked by the purchase of the Louisiana Territory from France (1803) and the Tripolitan War (1801-1805). A political philosopher, educator, and architect, Jefferson designed his own estate, Monticello, and buildings for the University of Virginia.

George Washington- American military leader and the first President of the United States (1789-1797). Commander of the American forces in the Revolutionary War (1775-1783), he presided over the Second Constitutional Convention (1787) and was elected President of the fledgling country (1789). He shunned partisan politics and in his farewell address (1796) warned against foreign involvement.

Benjamin Franklin - American public official, writer, scientist, and printer. After the success of his *Poor Richard's Almanac* (1732-1757), he entered politics and played a major part in the American Revolution. Franklin negotiated French support for the colonists, signed the Treaty of Paris (1783), and helped draft the Constitution (1787-1789). His numerous scientific and practical innovations include the lightning rod, bifocal spectacles, and a stove

Constitution- The fundamental law of the United States, framed in 1787, ratified in 1789, and variously amended since then

Bill of Rights- The first ten amendments to the U.S. Constitution, added in 1791 to protect certain rights of citizens

Growth and Expansion of the Republic

Know the origins of slavery and how it is addressed in the US Constitution. Know about the acquisition of Florida, Oregon, Texas, and California

Louisiana Purchase- A territory of the western United States extending from the Mississippi River to the Rocky Mountains between the Gulf of Mexico and the Canadian border. It was purchased from France on April 30, 1803, for $15 million and officially explored by the Lewis and Clark expedition (1804-1806).

Manifest Destiny- The 19th-century doctrine that the United States had the right and duty to expand throughout the North American continent.

Mexican War- A war (1846-1848) between the United States and Mexico, resulting in the cession by Mexico of lands now constituting all or most of the states of California, Arizona, New Mexico, Nevada, Utah, and Colorado

War of 1812- a war (1812-1814) between the United States and England which was trying to interfere with American trade with France

Monroe Doctrine- an American foreign policy opposing interference in the Western hemisphere from outside powers

Trail of Tears - the illegal removal by the United States government of the Cherokee of Georgia to what was called Indian Territory in 1838-39. Several other of the five civilized tribes had their own versions of the Trail of Tears, which were also called as such

Eli Whitney- American inventor and manufacturer whose invention of the cotton gin (1793) revolutionized the cotton industry. He also established the first factory to assemble muskets with interchangeable parts, marking the advent of modern mass production

Civil War- The war in the United States between the Union and the Confederacy from 1861 to 1865.

Know the abolitionist movement, the women's movement, the Fugitive slave act, and Dred Scott case.

Abraham Lincoln- The 16th President of the United States (1861-1865), who led the Union during the Civil War and emancipated slaves in the South (1863). He was assassinated shortly after the end of the war by John Wilkes Booth

Harriet Tubman- American abolitionist. Born a slave on a Maryland plantation, she escaped to the North in 1849 and became the most renowned conductor on the Underground Railroad, leading more than 300 slaves to freedom

William Lloyd Garrison- American abolitionist leader who founded and published *The Liberator* (1831-1865), an antislavery journal

Harriet Beecher Stowe- American writer whose antislavery novel *Uncle Tom's Cabin* (1852) had great political influence and advanced the cause of abolition

Gettysburg Address- A 3-minute address by Abraham Lincoln during the American Civil War (November 19, 1863) at the dedication of a national cemetery on the site of the Battle of Gettysburg

Emancipation Proclamation- An order issued during the Civil War by President Lincoln ending slavery in the Confederate states

Andrew Carnegie- Scottish-born American industrialist and philanthropist who amassed a fortune in the steel industry and donated millions of dollars for the benefit of the public

John D. Rockefeller- United States industrialist who made a fortune in the oil business and gave half of it away (1839-1937

Panama canal- a ship canal 40 miles long across the Isthmus of Panama built by the United States (1904-1914)

20th Century Developments and Transformations

Harlem Renaissance- originally called the New Negro Movement; the Harlem Renaissance was a literary and intellectual flowering that fostered a new black cultural identity in the 1920s and 1930s

Authors include:

Langston Hughes, Countee Cullen, and Zora Neale Hurston

Prohibition- a law forbidding the sale of alcoholic beverages; "in 1920 the 18th amendment to the Constitution established prohibition in the US"

Women's Suffrage- The movement for Women's suffrage, led by suffragists and suffragettes, was a social, economic and political reform movement aimed at extending equal suffrage, the right to vote to women, according to the one-man-one-vote principle.

The Great Depression- a time period during the 1930s when there was a worldwide economic depression and mass unemployment

The New Deal- The programs and policies to promote economic recovery and social reform introduced during the 1930s by President Franklin D. Roosevelt

Korean War- A conflict that lasted from 1950 to 1953 between North Korea, aided by China, and South Korea, aided by United Nations forces consisting primarily of U.S. troops

McCarthyism- The practice of publicizing accusations of political disloyalty or subversion with insufficient regard to evidence

The Decisions to drop atomic bombs on Nagasaki and Hiroshima

Desegregation- To open (a school or workplace, for example) to members of all races or ethnic groups, especially by force of law

Vietnam War- a protracted military conflict (1954-1975) between the Communist forces of North Vietnam supported by China and the Soviet Union and the non-Communist forces of South Vietnam supported by the United States.

Understand the rise of the consumer oriented society and changing demographic populations and how they play a role in society. Also understand the role of the development of computers and information technology.

Government and Civics
Nature and Purpose of Government

Government- The act or process of governing, especially the control and administration of public policy in a political unit

Government serves many purposes including: collective decision making and conflict resolution

Forms of Government

There are several forms of Government including:

Federalism
Parliamentary system
Constitutional structures

Unitary systems

United States Constitution

Separation of power between three branches of government:

Legislative Branch- made up of the Congress and government agencies, such as the Government Printing Office and Library of Congress that provide assistance to and support services for the Congress. Article I of the Constitution established this branch and gave Congress the power to make laws. Congress has two parts, the House of Representatives and the Senate

Judicial Branch- made up of the court system. The Supreme Court is the highest court in the land. Article III of the Constitution established this Court and all other Federal courts were created by Congress. Courts decide arguments about the meaning of laws, how they are applied, and whether they break the rules of the Constitution.

Executive Branch- makes sure that the laws of the United States are obeyed. The President of the United States is the head of the executive branch of government. This branch is very large so the President gets help from the Vice President, department heads (Cabinet members), and heads of independent agencies

Rights and Responsibilities of Citizens

US citizens have Freedom of speech, press, assembly, petition, religion, and privacy. We also have property rights, the right to choose one's work, the right to join or not join a labor union, and the right to apply for copyrights and patents

There are also legal obligations to abide by such as obey the law, pay taxes, and serve on jury.

Understand the process immigrants go through to become a US citizen.

Know Landmark Supreme Court Decisions such as:

Roe vs. Wade
Marbury vs. Madison
Plessy vs. Ferguson
Miranda vs. Arizona
Brown vs. Board of Education

State and Local Government

Know responsibilities of state and local government and the relationship between state government and federal government.

Behavioral Sciences (Anthropology, Sociology, and Psychology)

Anthropology- The scientific study of the origin, the behavior, and the physical, social, and cultural development of humans

Archaeology- The systematic study of past human life and culture by the recovery and examination of remaining material evidence, such as graves, buildings, tools, and pottery

Know how family patterns address basic human needs. Understand how human experience and cultural expression contribute to the development and transmission of culture.

Sociology

Sociology- The study of human social behavior, especially the study of the origins, organization, institutions, and development of human society

Understand the role of socialization in society and the effects that it has.

Social stratification- the condition of being arranged in social strata or classes

Social mobility- The movement or shifting of membership between or within social classes by individuals or by groups

Understand the terms stereotypes, bias, values, and ideals.

Psychology- The science that deals with mental processes and behavior

Know the following terms:

Behavioralism
Cognitive development
Character
Emotions
Physiological influences
Social Influences
Needs vs. Wants
Perception

Motives

Values

Individual

Learning

Human development and growth is broken into four stages: infancy, childhood,

adolescence, and adulthood. Also know about gender influences

Economics

The Market

Scarcity- Insufficiency of amount or supply; shortage

Cost- An amount paid or required in payment for a purchase

Resources- Something that can be used for support or help

Needs- A condition or situation in which something is required

Wants- To desire greatly; wish for

Opportunity Cost- cost in terms of foregone alternatives

Market- The business of buying and selling a specified commodity

Property- Something owned; a possession

Capital- Wealth in the form of money or property, used or accumulated in a

business by a person, partnership, or corporation

Price- The amount as of money or goods, asked for or given in exchange for

something else

Competition- Rivalry between two or more businesses striving for the same

customer or market

Supply- the amount at which a producer is willing and able to produce

Demand-the amount at which a buyer is willing and able to buy

Production- The act or process of producing

Consumption- The act or process of consuming

Inflation- A persistent increase in the level of consumer prices or a persistent

decline in the purchasing power of money, caused by an increase in available

currency and credit beyond the proportion of available goods and services

Recession- An extended decline in general business activity, typically three

consecutive quarters of falling real gross national product

Trade- The business of buying and selling commodities; commerce

Know the following institutions:

Labor unions
Corporation
Banks
Insurance Companies
Nonprofit institutions

Individuals and the Market

Employment- The work in which one is engaged; occupation

Unemployment- Out of work, especially involuntarily; jobless

Minimum Wage- The lowest wage, determined by law or contract that an employer may pay an employee for a specified job

Cost of living- The average cost of the basic necessities of life, such as food, shelter, and clothing

Know different types of marketing such as public relations, advertising, and customer service.

Be familiar with skills that good workers must possess.

Economics' effect of Population and Resources

Understand what natural, capital, and human resources are. Know what is meant by division of labor.

Government's role in economics and economics' impact on government

Know reasons why governments levy taxes such as military salaries, roads, schools, know the Government's role in maintaining the currency.

Federal Reserve- the central bank of the US; incorporates 12 Federal Reserve branch banks and all national banks and stated charted commercial banks and some trust companies

Consumer Price Index- An index of prices used to measure the change in the cost of basic goods and services in comparison with a fixed base period

Gross National Product- The total market value of all the goods and services produced by a nation during a specified period

Gross Domestic Product- The total market value of all the goods and services produced within the borders of a nation during a specified period

Economic Systems

Know the characteristics of the following:

Socialism
Capitalism
Communism
Command economies
Traditional economies
Free-market economies

International Economies

Imports- To bring or carry in from an outside source, especially to bring in (goods or materials) from a foreign country for trade or sale

Exports- To send or transport (a commodity, for example) abroad, especially for trade or sale

Tariffs- A list or system of duties imposed by a government on imported or exported goods

Quotas- A proportional share, as of goods, assigned to a group or to each member of a group; an allotment

Economics sanctions- Restrictions upon international trade and finance that one country imposes on another for political reasons.

Exchange rate- the charge for exchanging currency of one country for currency of another

Special Report: ITBS Secrets in Action
Sample Question from the Mathematics Test

For a certain board game, two dice are thrown to determine the number of spaces to move. One player throws the two dice and the same number comes up on each of the dice. What is the probability that the sum of the two numbers is 9?

A. 0

B. 1/6

C. 2/9

D. 1/2

Let's look at a few different methods and steps to solving this problem.

1. Create an Algebra Problem

While you might think that creating an algebra problem is the last thing that you would want to do, it actually can make the problem extremely simple.

Consider what you know about the problem. You know that both dice are going to roll the same number, but you don't know what that number is. Therefore, make the number "x" the unknown variable that you will need to solve for.

Since you have two dice that both would roll the same number, then you have "2x" or "two times x". Since the sum of the two dice needs to equal nine, that gives you "$2x = 9$".

Solving for x, you should first divide both sides by 2. This creates $2x/2 = 9/2$. The twos cancel out on the left side and you are have $x = 9/2$ or $x = 4.5$

You know that a dice can only roll an integer: 1, 2, 3, 4, 5, or 6, therefore 4.5 is an impossible roll. An impossible roll means that there is a zero possibility it would occur, making choice A, zero, correct.

2. Run Through the Possibilities for Doubles

You know that you have to have the same number on both dice that you roll. There are only so many combinations, so quickly run through them all.

You could roll:

Double 1's = 1 + 1 = 2
Double 2's = 2 + 2 = 4
Double 3's = 3 + 3 = 6
Double 4's = 4 + 4 = 8
Double 5's = 5 + 5 = 10
Double 6's = 6 + 6 = 12

Now go through and see which, if any, combinations give you a sum of 9. As you can see here, there aren't any. No combination of doubles gives you a sum of 9, making it a zero probability, and choice A correct.

3. Run Through the Possibilities for Nine

Just as there are only so many possibilities for rolling doubles, there are also only so many possibilities to roll a sum of nine. Quickly calculate all the possibilities, starting with the first die.

If you rolled a 1 with the first die, then the highest you could roll with the second is a 6. Since 1 + 6 = 7, there is no way that you can roll a sum of 9 if your first die rolls a 1.

If you rolled a 2 with the first die, then the highest you could roll with the second is a 6. Since 2 + 6 = 8, there is no way that you can roll a sum of 9 if your first die rolls a 2.

If you rolled a 3 with the first die, then you could roll a 6 with your other die and have a sum of 9. Since 3 + 6 = 9, this is a valid possibility.

If you rolled a 4 with the first die, then you could roll a 5 with your other die and have a sum of 9. Since 4 + 5 = 9, this is a valid possibility.

If you rolled a 5 with the first die, then you could roll a 4 with your other die and have a sum of 9. Since 5 + 4 = 9, this is a valid possibility.

If you rolled a 6 with the first die, then you could roll a 3 with your other die and have a sum of 9. Since 6 + 3 = 9, this is a valid possibility.

Now review all the possibilities that give you a combination of 9. You have: 3 + 6, 4 + 5, 5 + 4, and 6 + 3. These are the only combinations that will give you a sum of 9, and none of them are doubles. Therefore, there is a zero probability that doubles could give you a sum of 9, and choice A is correct.

4. Calculate the Odds

Quickly calculate the odds for just rolling a 9, without setting any restrictions that it has to be through doubles or anything else. You've seen in Method 3 that there are 4 ways that you can roll a sum of 9. Since you have two dice, each with 6 sides, there are a total of 36 different combinations that you could roll (6*6 = 36). Four of those thirty-six possibilities give you a sum of 9. Four possibilities of rolling a 9 out of thirty-six total possibilities = 4/36 = 1/9. So that means there is a 1/9 chance that would roll a 9, without any restrictions. Once you add restrictions, such as having to roll doubles, then your odds are guaranteed to go down and be less than 1/9. Since the odds have to be less than 1/9, the only answer choice that satisfies that requirement, is choice A, which is zero, making choice A correct.

Sample Question from the Reading Test

Alice Fletcher, the Margaret Mead of her day, assisted several American Indian nations that were threatened with removal from their land to the Indian Territory. She helped them in petitioning Congress for legal titles to their farms. When no response came from Washington, she went there herself to present their case.

According to the statement above, Alice Fletcher attempted to:

A. imitate the studies of Margaret Mead

B. obtain property rights for American Indians

C. protect the integrity of the Indian Territory

D. persuade Washington to expand the Indian Territory

Let's look at a couple of different methods of solving this problem.

1. Identify the key words in each answer choice. These are the nouns and verbs that are the most important words in the answer choice.

A. imitate, studies

B. obtain, property rights

C. protect, integrity

D. persuade, expand

Now try to match up each of the key words with the passage and see where they fit. You're trying to find synonyms between the key words in the answer choices and key words in the passage.

A. imitate – no matches; studies – no matches

B. obtain – no matches; property rights – matches with "legal titles" in sentence 2.

C. protect – no matches; integrity – no matches

D. persuade – matches with "petitioning" in sentence 2; expand – no matches

At this point there are only two choices that have any matches, choice B and D, and they both have matches with sentence 2. This is a good sign, because ITBS will often write two answer choices that are close. Having two answer choices pointing towards sentence 2 as containing the key to the passage (and no other answer choices pointing to any other sentences) is a strong indicator that sentence 2 is the most likely sentence in which to find the answer.

Now let's compare choice B and D and the unmatched key words. Choice B still has "obtain" which doesn't have a clear match, while choice D has "expand" which doesn't have a clear match. To get into the mindset of Alice Fletcher, ask yourself a quick series of questions related to sentence 2.

Sentence 2 states "She helped them in petitioning Congress for legal titles to their farms."

Ask yourself, "Why did she do that?"

Answer: The American Indian nations wanted legal title to their farms and didn't already have it.

Then ask yourself: "So what did Alice Fletcher do?"

Answer: "She tried to help them get the legal title to their farms they wanted."

Now you've suddenly got that match. "Obtain" matches with "get", so your above answer could read, "She tried to help them get (or obtain) the legal title to their farms they wanted."

2. Use a process of elimination.

A. imitate the studies of Margaret Mead – Margaret Mead is only mentioned as a point of historical reference. The passage makes no mention of Mead's studies, only that Alice Fletcher is similar to her.

B. obtain property rights for American Indians – The passage discusses how American Indians were threatened with removal from their land, but Alice Fletcher helped them get legal title, going all the way to Washington to press their case. This is the correct answer. "Obtain property rights for American Indians" is exactly what she fought for.

C. protect the integrity of the Indian Territory – Protecting the integrity of a territory or area deals with maintaining a status quo of a boundary or border. Yet boundaries and borders aren't even mentioned in this passage, only property rights. It wasn't a boundary that Alice Fletcher was fighting to maintain, but rather the right for the American Indians to even live on the land at all.

D. persuade Washington to expand the Indian Territory – At first, this sounds like a good answer choice. Alice Fletcher was trying to persuade Washington. The difference though is that she wasn't trying to persuade them to expand the Indian Territory but legitimize it, i.e. grant legal title. "Expand" suggests dealing with an increase in square mileage, not the ownership at stake – remember the American Indians were threatened with removal from the land, not fighting to increase the amount of land under their control.

Sample Question from the Science Test

Table 1

Length of 0.10 mm diameter aluminum wire(m)	Resistance (ohms) at 20° C
1	3.55
2	7.10
4	14.20
10	35.50

Based on the information in Table 1, one would predict that a 20 m length of aluminum wire with a 0.10 mm diameter would have a resistance of:

A. 16 ohms

B. 25 ohms

C. 34 ohms

D. 71 ohms

Let's look at a few different methods and steps to solving this problem.

1. Create a Proportion or Ratio

The first way you could approach this problem is by setting up a proportion or ratio. You will find that many of the problems on the ITBS can be solved using this simple technique. Usually whenever you have a given pair of numbers (this number goes with that number) and you are given a third number and asked to find what number would be its match, then you have a problem that can be converted into an easy proportion or ratio.

In this case you can take any of the pairs of numbers from Table 1. As an example, let's choose the second set of numbers (2 m and 7.10 ohms).

Form a question with the information you have at your disposal: 2 meters goes to 7.10 ohms as 20 meters (from the question) goes to which resistance?

From your ratio: 2m/7.10 ohms = 20m/x
"x" is used as the missing number that you will solve for.

Cross multiplication provides us with 2*x = 7.10*20 or 2x = 142.

Dividing both sides by 2 gives us 2x/2 = 142/2 or x = 71, making choice D correct.

2. Use Algebra

The question is asking for the resistance of a 20 m length of wire. The resistance is a function of the length of the wire, so you know that you could probably set up an algebra problem that would have 20 multiplied by some factor "x" that would give you your answer.

So, now you have 20*x = ?

But what exactly is "x"? If 20*x would give you the resistance of a 20 meter piece of wire, than 1*x would give you the resistance of a 1 meter piece of wire. Remember though, the table already told you the resistance of a 1 meter piece of wire – it's 3.55 ohms.

So, if 1*x = 3.55 ohms, then solving for "x" gives you x = 3.55 ohms.

Plugging your solution for "x" back into your initial equation of 20*x = ?, you now have 20*3.55 ohms = 71 ohms, making choice D correct.

3. Look for a Pattern

Much of the time you can get by with just looking for patterns on problems that provide you with a lot of different numbers. In this case, consider the provided table.

1 – 3.55
2 – 7.10
4 – 14.20
10 – 35.50

What patterns do you see in the above number sequences. It appears that when the number in the first column doubled from 1 to 2, the numbers in the second column doubled as well, going from 3.55 to 7.10. Further inspection shows that when the numbers in the first column doubled from 2 to 4, the numbers in the second column doubled again, going from 7.10 to 14.20. Now you've got a pattern, when the first column of numbers doubles, so does the second column.

Since the question asked about a resistance of 20, you should recognize that 20 is the double of 10. Since a length of 10 meant a resistance of 35.50 ohms, then doubling the length of 10 should double the resistance, making 71 ohms, or choice D, correct.

4. Use Logic

A method that works even faster than finding patterns or setting up equations is using simple logic. It appears that as the first number (the length of the wire) gets larger, so does the second number (the resistance).

Since the length of 10 (the largest length wire in the provided table) has a corresponding resistance of 35.50, then another length (such as 20 in the question) should have a length greater than 35.50. As you inspect the answer choices, there is only one answer choice that is greater than 35.50, which is choice D, making it correct.

Secret Key #1 – Guessing is not guesswork.

You probably know that guessing is a good idea on the ITBS- unlike other standardized tests, there is no penalty for getting a wrong answer. Even if you have no idea about a question, you still have a 20-25% chance of getting it right.

Most test takers do not understand the impact that proper guessing can have on their score. Unless you score extremely high, guessing will significantly contribute to your final score.

Monkeys Take the ITBS

What most test takers don't realize is that to insure that 20-25% chance, you have to guess randomly. If you put 20 monkeys in a room to take the ITBS, assuming they answered once per question and behaved themselves, on average they would get 20-25% of the questions correct. Put 20 test takers in the room, and the average will be much lower among guessed questions. Why?

1. ITBS intentionally writes deceptive answer choices that "look" right. A test taker has no idea about a question, so picks the "best looking" answer, which is often wrong. The monkey has no idea what looks good and what doesn't, so will consistently be lucky about 20-25% of the time.
2. Test takers will eliminate answer choices from the guessing pool based on a hunch or intuition. Simple but correct answers often get excluded, leaving a 0% chance of being correct. The monkey has no clue, and often gets lucky with the best choice.

This is why the process of elimination endorsed by most test courses is flawed and detrimental to your performance- test takers don't guess, they make an ignorant stab in the dark that is usually worse than random.

Success Strategy #1

Let me introduce one of the most valuable ideas of this course- the $5 challenge:

You only mark your "best guess" if you are willing to bet $5 on it.
You only eliminate choices from guessing if you are willing to bet $5 on it.

Why $5? Five dollars is an amount of money that is small yet not insignificant, and can really add up fast (20 questions could cost you $100). Likewise, each answer choice on one question of the ITBS will have a small impact on your overall score, but it can really add up to a lot of points in the end.

The process of elimination IS valuable. The following shows your chance of guessing it right:

If you eliminate this many choices:	0	1	2	3
Chance of getting it correct	25%	33%	50%	100%

However, if you accidentally eliminate the right answer or go on a hunch for an incorrect answer, your chances drop dramatically: to 0%. By guessing among all the answer choices, you are GUARANTEED to have a shot at the right answer.

That's why the $5 test is so valuable- if you give up the advantage and safety of a pure guess, it had better be worth the risk.

What we still haven't covered is how to be sure that whatever guess you make is truly random. Here's the easiest way:

Always pick the first answer choice among those remaining.

Such a technique means that you have decided, **before you see a single test question**, exactly how you are going to guess- and since the order of choices tells you nothing about which one is correct, this guessing technique is perfectly random.

Let's try an example-

A test taker encounters the following problem on the mathematics test:

What is the cosine of an angle in a right triangle that is 3 meters on the adjacent side, 5 meters on the hypotenuse, and 4 meters on the opposite side?

A. 1
B. 0.6
C. 0.8
D. 1.25

The test taker has a small idea about this question- he is pretty sure that cosine is opposite over hypotenuse, but he wouldn't bet $5 on it. He knows that cosine is "something" over hypotenuse, and since the hypotenuse is the largest number, he is willing to bet $5 on both choices A and D not being correct. So he is down to B and C. At this point, he guesses B, since B is the first choice remaining.

The test taker is correct by choosing B, since cosine is adjacent over hypotenuse. He only eliminated those choices he was willing to bet money on, AND he did not let his stale memories (often things not known definitely will get mixed up in the exact opposite arrangement in one's head) about the formula for cosine influence his guess. He blindly chose the first remaining choice, and was rewarded with the fruits of a random guess.

This section is not meant to scare you away from making educated guesses or eliminating choices- you just need to define when a choice is worth eliminating. The $5 test, along with a pre-defined random guessing strategy, is the best way to make sure you reap all of the benefits of guessing.

Specific Guessing Techniques

Slang

Scientific sounding answers are better than slang ones. In the answer choices below, choice B is much less scientific and is incorrect, while choice A is a scientific analytical choice and is correct.

Example:

A.) To compare the outcomes of the two different kinds of treatment.

B.) Because some subjects insisted on getting one or the other of the treatments.

Extreme Statements

Avoid wild answers that throw out highly controversial ideas that are proclaimed as established fact. Choice A is a radical idea and is incorrect. Choice B is a calm rational statement. Notice that Choice B does not make a definitive, uncompromising stance, using a hedge word "if" to provide wiggle room.

Example:

A.) Bypass surgery should be discontinued completely.

B.) Medication should be used instead of surgery for patients who have not had a heart attack if they suffer from mild chest pain and mild coronary artery blockage.

Similar Answer Choices

When you have two answer choices that are direct opposites, one of them is usually the correct answer.

Example:

A.) Paragraph 1 described the author's reasoning about the influence of his childhood on his adult life.

B.) Paragraph 2 described the author's reasoning about the influence of his childhood on his adult life.

These two answer choices are very similar and fall into the same family of answer choices. A family of answer choices is when two or three answer choices are very similar. Often two will be opposites and one may show an equality.

Example:

A.) Operation I or Operation II can be conducted at equal cost

B.) Operation I would be less expensive than Operation II

C.) Operation II would be less expensive than Operation I

D.) Neither Operation I nor Operation II would be effective at preventing the spread of cancer.

Note how the first three choices are all related. They all ask about a cost comparison. Beware of immediately recognizing choices B and C as opposites and choosing one of those two. Choice A is in the same family of questions and should be considered as well. However, choice D is not in the same family of questions. It has nothing to do with cost and can be discounted in most cases.

Hedging

When asked for a conclusion that may be drawn, look for critical "hedge" phrases, such as likely, may, can, will often, sometimes, etc, often, almost, mostly, usually, generally, rarely, sometimes. Question writers insert these hedge phrases to cover every possibility. Often an answer will be wrong simply because it leaves no room for exception. Avoid answer choices that have definitive words like "exactly," and "always".

Summary of Guessing Techniques

1. Eliminate as many choices as you can by using the $5 test. Use the common guessing strategies to help in the elimination process, but only eliminate choices that pass the $5 test.

2. Among the remaining choices, only pick your "best guess" if it passes the $5 test.

3. Otherwise, guess randomly by picking the first remaining choice.

Secret Key #2 – Practice Smarter, Not Harder

Many test takers delay the test preparation process because they dread the awful amounts of practice time they think necessary to succeed on the test. We have refined an effective method that will take you only a fraction of the time.

There are a number of "obstacles" in your way on the ITBS. Among these are answering questions, finishing in time, and mastering test-taking strategies. All must be executed on the day of the test at peak performance, or your score will suffer. The ITBS is a mental marathon that has a large impact on your future.

Just like a marathon runner, it is important to work your way up to the full challenge. So first you just worry about questions, and then time, and finally strategy:

Success Strategy #2

1. Find a good source for ITBS practice tests.
2. If you are willing to make a larger time investment, consider using more than one study guide- often the different approaches of multiple authors will help you "get" difficult concepts.
3. Take a practice test with no time constraints, with all study helps "open book." Take your time with questions and focus on the strategies.
4. Take another test, this time with time constraints, with all study helps "open book."
5. Take a final practice test with no open material and time limits. This will be the real test of if you know the material.

If you have time to take more practice tests, just repeat step 5. By gradually exposing yourself to the full rigors of the test environment, you will condition your mind to the stress of test day and maximize your success.

Secret Key #3 – Prepare, Don't Procrastinate

Let me state an obvious fact: if you take the ITBS three times, you will get three different scores. This is due to the way you feel on test day, the level of preparedness you have, and, despite ITBS's claims to the contrary, some tests WILL be easier for you than others.

Since so much depends on your score, you should maximize your chances of success. In order to maximize the likelihood of success, you've got to prepare in advance. This means taking practice tests and spending time learning the information and test taking strategies you will need to succeed.

You can always retake the test more than once, but when you go to take the ITBS, be prepared, be focused, and do your best the first time!

Secret Key #4 – Test Yourself

Everyone knows that time is money. There is no need to spend too much of your time or too little of your time preparing for the ITBS. You should only spend as much of your precious time preparing as is necessary for you to pass it.

Success Strategy #4

Once you have taken a practice test under real conditions of time constraints, then you will know if you are ready for the test or not.

If you have scored extremely high the first time that you take the practice test, then there is not much point in spending countless hours studying. You are already there.

If you are close to a passing score, whether above or below, then you should spend a moderate amount of time studying. Benchmark your abilities by retaking practice tests and seeing how much you have improved. Once you score high enough to have a comfortable margin between your score and a passing, then you are ready.

If you have scored well below where you need, then knuckle down and begin studying in earnest. Check your improvement regularly through the use of practice tests under real conditions. Above all, don't worry, panic, or give up. The key is perseverance!

Then, when you go to take the ITBS, be prepared, be focused, and do your best. Remain confident and remember how well you did on the practice tests. If you can score a passing score on a practice test, then you can do the same on the real thing.

General Strategies

The most important thing you can do is to ignore your fears and jump into the test immediately- do not be overwhelmed by any strange-sounding terms. You have to jump into the test like jumping into a pool- all at once is the easiest way.

Make Predictions

As you read and understand the question, try to guess what the answer will be. Remember that several of the answer choices are wrong, and once you begin reading them, your mind will immediately become cluttered with answer choices designed to throw you off. Your mind is typically the most focused immediately after you have read the question and digested its contents. If you can, try to predict what the correct answer will be. You may be surprised at what you can predict.

Quickly scan the choices and see if your prediction is in the listed answer choices. If it is, then you can be quite confident that you have the right answer. It still won't hurt to check the other answer choices, but most of the time, you've got it!

Answer the Question

It may seem obvious to only pick answer choices that answer the question, but the test writers can create some excellent answer choices that are wrong. Don't pick an answer just because it sounds right, or you believe it to be true. It MUST answer the question. Once you've made your selection, always go back and check it against the question and make sure that you didn't misread the question, and the answer choice does answer the question posed.

Benchmark

After you read the first answer choice, decide if you think it sounds correct or not. If it doesn't, move on to the next answer choice. If it does, mentally mark that answer choice. This doesn't mean that you've definitely selected it as your answer choice, it just means that it's the best you've seen thus far. Go ahead and read the next choice. If the next choice is worse than the one you've already selected, keep going to the next answer choice. If the next choice is better than the choice you've already selected, mentally mark the new answer choice as your best guess.

The first answer choice that you select becomes your standard. Every other answer choice must be benchmarked against that standard. That choice is correct until proven otherwise by another answer choice beating it out. Once you've decided that no other answer choice seems as good, do one final check to ensure that your answer choice answers the question posed.

Valid Information

Don't discount any of the information provided in the question. Every piece of information may be necessary to determine the correct answer. None of the information in the question is there to throw you off (while the answer choices will certainly have information to throw you off). If two seemingly unrelated topics are discussed, don't ignore either. You can be confident there is a relationship, or it wouldn't be included in the question, and you are probably going to have to determine what is that relationship to find the answer.

Avoid "Fact Traps"

Don't get distracted by a choice that is factually true. Your search is for the answer that answers the question. Stay focused and don't fall for an answer that is true but incorrect. Always go back to the question and make sure you're choosing an answer that actually answers the question and is not just a true statement. An answer can be factually correct, but it MUST answer the question asked. Additionally, two answers can both be seemingly correct, so be sure to read all of the answer choices, and make sure that you get the one that BEST answers the question.

Milk the Question

Some of the questions may throw you completely off. They might deal with a subject you have not been exposed to, or one that you haven't reviewed in years.

While your lack of knowledge about the subject will be a hindrance, the question itself can give you many clues that will help you find the correct answer. Read the question carefully and look for clues. Watch particularly for adjectives and nouns describing difficult terms or words that you don't recognize. Regardless of if you completely understand a word or not, replacing it with a synonym either provided or one you more familiar with may help you to understand what the questions are asking. Rather than wracking your mind about specific detailed information concerning a difficult term or word, try to use mental substitutes that are easier to understand.

The Trap of Familiarity

Don't just choose a word because you recognize it. On difficult questions, you may not recognize a number of words in the answer choices. The test writers don't put "make-believe" words on the test; so don't think that just because you only recognize all the words in one answer choice means that answer choice must be correct. If you only recognize words in one answer choice, then focus on that one. Is it correct? Try your best to determine if it is correct. If it is, that is great, but if it doesn't, eliminate it. Each word and answer choice you eliminate increases your chances of getting the question correct, even if you then have to guess among the unfamiliar choices.

Eliminate Answers

Eliminate choices as soon as you realize they are wrong. But be careful! Make sure you consider all of the possible answer choices. Just because one appears right, doesn't mean that the next one won't be even better! The test writers will usually put more than one good answer choice for every question, so read all of them. Don't worry if you are stuck between two that seem right. By getting down to just two remaining possible choices, your odds are now 50/50. Rather than wasting too much time, play the odds. You are guessing, but guessing wisely, because you've been able to knock out some of the answer choices that you know are wrong. If you are eliminating choices and realize that the last answer choice you are left with is also obviously wrong, don't panic. Start over and consider each choice again. There may easily be something that you missed the first time and will realize on the second pass.

Tough Questions

If you are stumped on a problem or it appears too hard or too difficult, don't waste time. Move on! Remember though, if you can quickly check for obviously incorrect answer choices, your chances of guessing correctly are greatly improved. Before you completely give up, at least try to knock out a couple of possible answers. Eliminate what you can and then guess at the remaining answer choices before moving on.

Brainstorm

If you get stuck on a difficult question, spend a few seconds quickly brainstorming. Run through the complete list of possible answer choices. Look at each choice and ask yourself, "Could this answer the question satisfactorily?" Go through each answer choice and consider it independently of the other. By systematically going through all possibilities, you may find something that you would otherwise overlook. Remember that when you get stuck, it's important to try to keep moving.

Read Carefully

Understand the problem. Read the question and answer choices carefully. Don't miss the question because you misread the terms. You have plenty of time to read each question thoroughly and make sure you understand what is being asked. Yet a happy medium must be attained, so don't waste too much time. You must read carefully, but efficiently.

Face Value

When in doubt, use common sense. Always accept the situation in the problem at face value. Don't read too much into it. These problems will not require you to make huge leaps of logic. The test writers aren't trying to throw you off with a cheap trick. If you have to go beyond creativity and make a leap of logic in order to have an answer choice answer the question, then you should look at the other answer choices. Don't overcomplicate the problem by creating theoretical relationships or explanations that will warp time or space. These are normal problems rooted in reality. It's just that the applicable relationship or explanation may not be readily apparent and you have to figure things out. Use your common sense to interpret anything that isn't clear.

Prefixes

If you're having trouble with a word in the question or answer choices, try dissecting it. Take advantage of every clue that the word might include. Prefixes and suffixes can be a huge help. Usually they allow you to determine a basic meaning. Pre- means before, post- means after, pro - is positive, de- is negative. From these prefixes and suffixes, you can get an idea of the general meaning of the word and try to put it into context. Beware though of any traps. Just because con is the opposite of pro, doesn't necessarily mean congress is the opposite of progress!

Hedge Phrases

Watch out for critical "hedge" phrases, such as likely, may, can, will often, sometimes, often, almost, mostly, usually, generally, rarely, sometimes. Question writers insert these hedge phrases to cover every possibility. Often an answer choice will be wrong simply because it leaves no room for exception. Avoid answer choices that have definitive words like "exactly," and "always".

Switchback Words

Stay alert for "switchbacks". These are the words and phrases frequently used to alert you to shifts in thought. The most common switchback word is "but". Others include although, however, nevertheless, on the other hand, even though, while, in spite of, despite, regardless of.

New Information

Correct answer choices will rarely have completely new information included. Answer choices typically are straightforward reflections of the material asked about and will directly relate to the question. If a new piece of information is included in an answer choice that doesn't even seem to relate to the topic being asked about, then that answer choice is likely incorrect. All of the information needed to answer the question is usually provided for you, and so you should not have to make guesses that are unsupported or choose answer choices that require unknown information that cannot be reasoned on its own.

Time Management

On technical questions, don't get lost on the technical terms. Don't spend too much time on any one question. If you don't know what a term means, then since you don't have a dictionary, odds are you aren't going to get much further. You should immediately recognize terms as whether or not you know them. If you don't, work with the other clues that you have, the other answer choices and terms provided, but don't waste too much time trying to figure out a difficult term.

Contextual Clues

Look for contextual clues. An answer can be right but not correct. The contextual clues will help you find the answer that is most right and is correct. Understand the context in which a phrase or statement is made. This will help you make important distinctions.

Don't Panic

Panicking will not answer any questions for you. Therefore, it isn't helpful. When you first see the question, if your mind goes blank, take a deep breath. Force yourself to mechanically go through the steps of solving the problem and using the strategies you've learned.

Pace Yourself

Don't get clock fever. It's easy to be overwhelmed when you're looking at a page full of questions, your mind is full of random thoughts and feeling confused, and the clock is ticking down faster than you would like. Calm down and maintain the pace that you have set for yourself. As long as you are on track by monitoring your pace, you are guaranteed to have enough time for yourself. When you get to the last few minutes of the test, it may seem like you won't have enough time left, but if you only have as many questions as you should have left at that point, then you're right on track!

Answer Selection

The best way to pick an answer choice is to eliminate all of those that are wrong, until only one is left and confirm that is the correct answer. Sometimes though, an answer choice may immediately look right. Be careful! Take a second to make sure that the other choices are not equally obvious. Don't make a hasty mistake. There are only two times that you should stop before checking other answers. First is when you are positive that the answer choice you have selected is correct. Second is when time is almost out and you have to make a quick guess!

Check Your Work

Since you will probably not know every term listed and the answer to every question, it is important that you get credit for the ones that you do know. Don't miss any questions through careless mistakes. If at all possible, try to take a second to look back over your answer selection and make sure you've selected the correct answer choice and haven't made a costly careless mistake (such as marking an answer choice that you didn't mean to mark). This quick double check should more than pay for itself in caught mistakes for the time it costs.

Beware of Directly Quoted Answers

Sometimes an answer choice will repeat word for word a portion of the question or reference section. However, beware of such exact duplication – it may be a trap! More than likely, the correct choice will paraphrase or summarize a point, rather than being exactly the same wording.

Slang

Scientific sounding answers are better than slang ones. An answer choice that begins "To compare the outcomes..." is much more likely to be correct than one that begins "Because some people insisted..."

Extreme Statements

Avoid wild answers that throw out highly controversial ideas that are proclaimed as established fact. An answer choice that states the "process should be used in certain situations, if..." is much more likely to be correct than one that states the "process should be discontinued completely." The first is a calm rational statement and doesn't even make a definitive, uncompromising stance, using a hedge word "if" to provide wiggle room, whereas the second choice is a radical idea and far more extreme.

Answer Choice Families

When you have two or more answer choices that are direct opposites or parallels, one of them is usually the correct answer. For instance, if one answer choice states "x increases" and another answer choice states "x decreases" or "y increases," then those two or three answer choices are very similar in construction and fall into the same family of answer choices. A family of answer choices is when two or three answer choices are very similar in construction, and yet often have a directly opposite meaning. Usually the correct answer choice will be in that family of answer choices. The "odd man out" or answer choice that doesn't seem to fit the parallel construction of the other answer choices is more likely to be incorrect.

Special Report: How to Overcome Your Fear of Math

If this article started by saying "Math," many of us would feel a shiver crawl up our spines, just by reading that simple word. Images of torturous years in those crippling desks of the math classes can become so vivid to our consciousness that we can almost smell those musty textbooks, and see the smudges of the #2 pencils on our fingers.

If you are still a student, feeling the impact of these sometimes overwhelming classroom sensations, you are not alone if you get anxious at just the thought of taking that compulsory math course. Does your heart beat just that much faster when you have to split the bill for lunch among your friends with a group of your friends? Do you truly believe that you simply don't have the brain for math? Certainly you're good at other things, but math just simply isn't one of them? Have you ever avoided activities, or other school courses because they appear to involve mathematics, with which you're simply not comfortable?

If any one or more of these "symptoms" can be applied to you, you could very well be suffering from a very real condition called "Math Anxiety."

It's not at all uncommon for people to think that they have some sort of math disability or allergy, when in actuality, their block is a direct result of the way in which they were taught math!

In the late 1950's with the dawning of the space age, New Math - a new "fuzzy math" reform that focuses on higher-order thinking, conceptual understanding and solving problems - took the country by storm. It's now becoming ever more clear that teachers were not supplied with the correct, practical and effective way in which they should be teaching new math so that students will understand the methods comfortably. So is it any wonder that so many students struggled so deeply, when their teachers were required to change their entire math systems without the foundation of proper training? Even if you have not been personally, directly affected by that precise event, its impact is still as rampant as ever.

Basically, the math teachers of today are either the teachers who began teaching the new math in the first place (without proper training) or they are the students of the math teachers who taught new math without proper training. Therefore, unless they had a unique, exceptional teacher, their primary, consistent examples of teaching math have been teachers using methods that are not conducive to the general understanding of the entire class. This explains why your discomfort (or fear) of math is not at all rare.

It is very clear why being called up to the chalk board to solve a math problem is such a common example of a terrifying situation for students - and it has very little to do with a fear of being in front of the class. Most of us have had a minimum of one humiliating experience while standing with chalk dusted fingers, with the eyes of every math student piercing through us. These are the images that haunt us all the way through adulthood. But it does not mean that we cannot learn math. It just means that we could be developing a solid case of math anxiety.

But what exactly is math anxiety? It's an very strong emotional sensation of anxiety, panic, or fear that people feel when they think about or must apply their ability to understand mathematics. Sufferers of math anxiety frequently believe that they are incapable of doing activities or taking classes that involve math skills. In fact, some people with math anxiety have developed such a fear that it has become a phobia; aptly named math phobia.

The incidence of math anxiety, especially among college students, but also among high school students, has risen considerably over the last 10 years, and currently this increase shows no signs of slowing down. Frequently students will even chose their college majors and programs based specifically on how little math will be compulsory for the completion of the degree.

The prevalence of math anxiety has become so dramatic on college campuses that many of these schools have special counseling programs that are designed to assist math anxious students to deal with their discomfort and their math problems.

Math anxiety itself is not an intellectual problem, as many people have been lead to believe; it is, in fact, an emotional problem that stems from improper math teaching techniques that have slowly built and reinforced these feelings. However, math anxiety can result in an intellectual problem when its symptoms interfere with a person's ability to learn and understand math.

The fear of math can cause a sort of "glitch" in the brain that can cause an otherwise clever person to stumble over even the simplest of math problems. A study by Dr. Mark H. Ashcraft of Cleveland State University in Ohio showed that college students who usually perform well, but who suffer from math anxiety, will suffer from fleeting lapses in their working memory when they are asked to perform even the most basic mental arithmetic. These same issues regarding memory were not present in the same students when they were required to answer questions that did not involve numbers. This very clearly demonstrated that the memory phenomenon is quite specific to only math.

So what exactly is it that causes this inhibiting math anxiety? Unfortunately it is not as simple as one answer, since math anxiety doesn't have one specific cause.

Frequently math anxiety can result of a student's either negative experience or embarrassment with math or a math teacher in previous years.

These circumstances can prompt the student to believe that he or she is somehow deficient in his or her math abilities. This belief will consistently lead to a poor performance in math tests and courses in general, leading only to confirm the beliefs of the student's inability. This particular phenomenon is referred to as the "self-fulfilling prophecy" by the psychological community. Math anxiety will result in poor performance, rather than it being the other way around.

Dr. Ashcraft stated that math anxiety is a "It's a learned, almost phobic, reaction to math," and that it is not only people prone to anxiety, fear, or panic who can develop math anxiety. The image alone of doing math problems can send the blood pressure and heart rate to race, even in the calmest person.

The study by Dr. Ashcraft and his colleague Elizabeth P. Kirk, discovered that students who suffered from math anxiety were frequently stumped by issues of even the most basic math rules, such as "carrying over" a number, when performing a sum, or "borrowing" from a number when doing a subtraction. Lapses such as this occurred only on working memory questions involving numbers.

To explain the problem with memory, Ashcraft states that when math anxiety begins to take its effect, the sufferer experiences a rush of thoughts, leaving little room for the focus required to perform even the simplest of math problems. He stated that "you're draining away the energy you need for solving the problem by worrying about it."

The outcome is a "vicious cycle," for students who are sufferers of math anxiety. As math anxiety is developed, the fear it promotes stands in the way of learning, leading to a decrease in self-confidence in the ability to perform even simple arithmetic.

A large portion of the problem lies in the ways in which math is taught to students today. In the US, students are frequently taught the rules of math, but rarely will they learn why a specific approach to a math problems work. Should students be provided with a foundation of "deeper understanding" of math, it may prevent the development of phobias.

Another study that was published in the Journal of Experimental Psychology by Dr. Jamie Campbell and Dr. Qilin Xue of the University of Saskatchewan in Saskatoon, Canada, reflected the same concepts. The researchers in this study looked at university students who were educated in Canada and China, discovering that the Chinese students could generally outperform the Canadian-educated students when it came to solving complex math problems involving procedural knowledge - the ability to know how to solve a math problem, instead of simply having ideas memorized.

A portion of this result seemed to be due to the use of calculators within both elementary and secondary schools; while Canadians frequently used them, the Chinese students did not.

However, calculators were not the only issue. Since Chinese-educated students also outperformed Canadian-educated students in complex math, it is suggested that cultural factors may also have an impact. However, the short-cut of using the calculator may hinder the development of the problem solving skills that are key to performing well in math.

Though it is critical that students develop such fine math skills, it is easier said than done. It would involve an overhaul of the training among all elementary and secondary educators, changing the education major in every college.

Math Myths

One problem that contributes to the progression of math anxiety, is the belief of many math myths. These erroneous math beliefs include the following:

Men are better in math than women - however, research has failed to demonstrate that there is any difference in math ability between the sexes. There is a single best way to solve a math problem - however, the majority of math problems can be solved in a number of different ways. By saying that there is only one way to solve a math problem, the thinking and creative skills of the student are held back.

Some people have a math mind, and others do not - in truth, the majority of people have much more potential for their math capabilities than they believe of themselves.

It is a bad thing to count by using your fingers - counting by using fingers has actually shown that an understanding of arithmetic has been established. People who are skilled in math can do problems quickly in their heads - in actuality, even math professors will review their example problems before they teach them in their classes.

The anxieties formed by these myths can frequently be perpetuated by a range of mind games that students seem to play with themselves. These math mind games include the following beliefs:

I don't perform math fast enough - actually everyone has a different rate at which he or she can learn. The speed of the solving of math problems is not important as long as the student can solve it.

I don't have the mind for math - this belief can inhibit a student's belief in him or herself, and will therefore interfere with the student's real ability to learn math.

I got the correct answer, but it was done the wrong way - there is no single best way to complete a math problem. By believing this, a student's creativity and overall understanding of math is hindered.

If I can get the correct answer, then it is too simple - students who suffer from math anxiety frequently belittle their own abilities when it comes to their math capabilities.

Math is unrelated to my "real" life - by freeing themselves of the fear of math, math anxiety sufferers are only limiting their choices and freedoms for the rest of their life.

Fortunately, there are many ways to help those who suffer from math anxiety. Since math anxiety is a learned, psychological response to doing or thinking about math, that interferes with the sufferer's ability to understand and perform math, it is not at all a reflection of the sufferer's true math sills and abilities.

Helpful Strategies

Many strategies and therapies have been developed to help students to overcome their math anxious responses. Some of these helpful strategies include the following:

Reviewing and learning basic arithmetic principles, techniques and methods. Frequently math anxiety is a result of the experience of many students with early negative situations, and these students have never truly developed a strong base in basic arithmetic, especially in the case of multiplication and fractions. Since math is a discipline that is built on an accumulative foundation, where the concepts are built upon gradually from simpler concepts, a student who has not achieved a solid basis in arithmetic will experience difficulty in learning higher order math. Taking a remedial math course, or a short math course that focuses on arithmetic can often make a considerable difference in reducing the anxious response that math anxiety sufferers have with math.

Becoming aware of any thoughts, actions and feelings that are related to math and responses to math. Math anxiety has a different effect on different students. Therefore it is very important to become familiar with any reactions that the math anxiety sufferer may have about him/herself and the situation when math has been encountered. If the sufferer becomes aware of any irrational or unrealistic thoughts, it's possible to better concentrate on replacing these thoughts with more positive and realistic ones.

Find help! Math anxiety, as we've mentioned, is a learned response, that is reinforced repeatedly over a period of time, and is therefore not something that can be eliminated instantaneously. Students can more effectively reduce their anxious responses with the help of many different services that are readily available. Seeking the assistance of a psychologist or counselor, especially one with a specialty in math anxiety, can assist the sufferer in performing an analysis of his/her psychological response to math, as well as learning anxiety management skills, and developing effective coping strategies. Other great tools are tutors, classes that teach better abilities to take better notes in math class, and other math learning aids.

Learning the mathematic vocabulary will instantly provide a better chance for understanding new concepts. One major issue among students is the lack of understanding of the terms and vocabulary that are common jargon within math classes. Typically math classes will utilize words in a completely different way from the way in which they are utilized in all other subjects. Students easily mistake their lack of understanding the math terms with their mathematical abilities.

Learning anxiety reducing techniques and methods for anxiety management. Anxiety greatly interferes with a student's ability to concentrate, think clearly, pay attention, and remember new concepts. When these same students can learn to relax, using anxiety management techniques, the student can regain his or her ability to control his or her emotional and physical symptoms of anxiety that interfere with the capabilities of mental processing.

Working on creating a positive overall attitude about mathematics. Looking at math with a positive attitude will reduce anxiety through the building of a positive attitude.

Learning to self-talk in a positive way. Pep talking oneself through a positive self talk can greatly assist in overcoming beliefs in math myths or the mind games that may be played. Positive self-talking is an effective way to replace the negative thoughts - the ones that create the anxiety. Even if the sufferer doesn't believe the statements at first, it plants a positive seed in the subconscious, and allows a positive outlook to grow.

Beyond this, students should learn effective math class, note taking and studying techniques. Typically, the math anxious students will avoid asking questions to save themselves from embarrassment. They will sit in the back of classrooms, and refrain from seeking assistance from the professor. Moreover, they will put off studying for math until the very last moment, since it causes them such substantial discomfort. Alone, or a combination of these negative behaviors work only to reduce the anxiety of the students, but in reality, they are actually building a substantially more intense anxiety.

There are many different positive behaviors that can be adopted by math anxious students, so that they can learn to better perform within their math classes.

Sit near the front of the class. This way, there will be fewer distractions, and there will be more of a sensation of being a part of the topic of discussion. If any questions arise, ASK! If one student has a question, then there are certain to be others who have the same question but are too nervous to ask - perhaps because they have not yet learned how to deal with their own math anxiety.

Seek extra help from the professor after class or during office hours.

Prepare, prepare, prepare - read textbook material before the class, do the homework and work out any problems available within the textbook. Math skills are developed through practice and repetition, so the more practice and repetition, the better the math skills.

Review the material once again after class, to repeat it another time, and to reinforce the new concepts that were learned.

Beyond these tactics that can be taken by the students themselves, teachers and parents need to know that they can also have a large impact on the reduction of math anxiety within students.

As parents and teachers, there is a natural desire to help students to learn and understand how they will one day utilize different math techniques within their everyday lives. But when the student or teacher displays the symptoms of a person who has had nightmarish memories regarding math, where hesitations then develop in the instruction of students, these fears are automatically picked up by the students and commonly adopted as their own.

However, it is possible for teachers and parents to move beyond their own fears to better educate students by overcoming their own hesitations and learning to enjoy math.

Begin by adopting the outlook that math is a beautiful, imaginative or living thing. Of course, we normally think of mathematics as numbers that can be added or subtracted, multiplied or divided, but that is simply the beginning of it.

By thinking of math as something fun and imaginative, parents and teachers can teach children different ways to manipulate numbers, for example in balancing a checkbook. Parents rarely tell their children that math is everywhere around us; in nature, art, and even architecture. Usually, this is because they were never shown these relatively simple connections. But that pattern can break very simply through the participation of parents and teachers.

The beauty and hidden wonders of mathematics can easily be emphasized through a focus that can open the eyes of students to the incredible mathematical patterns that arise everywhere within the natural world. Observations and discussions can be made into things as fascinating as spider webs, leaf patterns, sunflowers and even coastlines. This makes math not only beautiful, but also inspiring and (dare we say) fun!

Pappas Method

For parents and teachers to assist their students in discovering the true wonders of mathematics, the techniques of Theoni Pappas can easily be applied, as per her popular and celebrated book "Fractals, Googols and Other Mathematical Tales." Pappas used to be a math phobia sufferer and created a fascinating step-by-step program for parents and teachers to use in order to teach students the joy of math.

Her simple, constructive step-by-step program goes as follows:

Don't let your fear of math come across to your kids - Parents must be careful not to perpetuate the mathematical myth - that math is only for specially talented "math types." Strive not to make comments like; "they don't like math" or "I have never been good at math." When children overhear comments like these from their primary role models they begin to dread math before even considering a chance of experiencing its wonders. It is important to encourage your children to read and explore the rich world of mathematics, and to practice mathematics without imparting negative biases.

Don't immediately associate math with computation (counting) - It is very important to realize that math is not just numbers and computations, but a realm of exciting ideas that touch every part of our lives -from making a telephone call to how the hair grows on someone's head. Take your children outside and point out real objects that display math concepts. For example, show them the symmetry of a leaf or angles on a building. Take a close look at the spirals in a spider web or intricate patterns of a snowflake.

Help your child understand why math is important - Math improves problem solving, increases competency and should be applied in different ways. It's the same as reading. You can learn the basics of reading without ever enjoying a novel. But, where's the excitement in that? With math, you could stop with the basics. But why when there is so much more to be gained by a fuller Understanding? Life is so much more enriching when we go beyond the basics. Stretch your children's minds to become involved in mathematics in ways that will not only be practical but also enhance their lives.

Make math as "hands on" as possible - Mathematicians participate in mathematics. To really experience math encourage your child to dig in and tackle problems in creative ways. Help them learn how to manipulate numbers using concrete references they understand as well as things they can see or touch. Look for patterns everywhere, explore shapes and symmetries. How many octagons do you see each day on the way to the grocery store? Play math puzzles and games and then encourage your child to try to invent their own. And, whenever possible, help your child realize a mathematical conclusion with real and tangible results. For example, measure out a full glass of juice with a measuring cup and then ask your child to drink half. Measure what is left. Does it measure half of a cup?

Read books that make math exciting:

Fractals, Googols and Other Mathematical Tales introduces an animated cat who explains fractals, tangrams and other mathematical concepts you've probably never heard of to children in terms they can understand. This book can double as a great text book by using one story per lesson.

A Wrinkle in Time is a well-loved classic, combining fantasy and science.

The Joy of Mathematics helps adults explore the beauty of mathematics that is all around.

The Math Curse is an amusing book for 4-8 year olds.

The Gnarly Gnews is a free, humorous bi-monthly newsletter on mathematics.

The Phantom Tollbooth is an Alice in Wonderland-style adventure into the worlds of words and numbers.

Use the internet to help your child explore the fascinating world of mathematics. Web Math provides a powerful set of math-solvers that gives you instant answers to the stickiest problems.

Math League has challenging math materials and contests for fourth grade and above.

Silver Burdett Ginn Mathematics offers Internet-based math activities for grades K-6.

The Gallery of Interactive Geometry is full of fascinating, interactive geometry activities.

Math is very much like a language of its own. And like any second language, it will get rusty if it is not practiced enough. For that reason, students should always be looking into new ways to keep understanding and brushing up on their math skills, to be certain that foundations do not crumble, inhibiting the learning of new levels of math.

There are many different books, services and websites that have been developed to take the fear out of math, and to help even the most uncertain student develop self confidence in his or her math capabilities.

There is no reason for math or math classes to be a frightening experience, nor should it drive a student crazy, making them believe that they simply don't have the "math brain" that is needed to solve certain problems.

There are friendly ways to tackle such problems and it's all a matter of dispelling myths and creating a solid math foundation.

Concentrate on re-learning the basics and feeling better about yourself in math, and you'll find that the math brain you've always wanted, was there all along.